KU-710-429

318615

Potato

Lyndsay and Patrick Mikanowski

Photography Grant Symon

Potato

Grub Street • London

Contents

Page 74 | 53 Potato Fanatics

Simple Pleasures

Classic Tastes

New and Enticing

Page 186 | Potato Notebook

Foreword

Man's relationship with nature is a source of goodness. It is the fruit of labours humans have performed since the dawn of time. The course of nature is affected by our efforts to shape it, and we destroy natural environments while helping to develop others. We reap the benefits and suffer the ravages.

Hunters, gatherers, farmers, gardeners, scientists or artists, hikers or cooks all observe, sort and order the natural environment, then adapt their behaviour according to what they learn and surmise. When this interaction is successful – that is, when it produces results and mutual satisfaction – humans live alongside nature in a harmony that is evident in both the people and the surrounding flora and fauna. This harmony rests on a series of choices, which, provided they are made with respect for the voice of experience, can lead to a feeling of authenticity.

Among the domesticated plants, the edible ones, and particularly those that constitute staples, are of central importance and determine people's health and prosperity.

Today, the potato is consumed across the globe and takes fourth place after rice, wheat and maize for the number of harvested tons. This is because it is a source of goodness. Nevertheless, it continues to lag far behind cereal crops.

Yet its future is more than assured. It is set to become the edible plant most suited to sustaining a planet where millions of men, women and children cannot eat their fill. A few shadows first need to be dispersed: currently, no other cultivated plant is so chemical-dependent.

The story of how the potato came to Europe remains steeped in myth. This book does not attempt to retell tales that are amply recorded elsewhere, with all their attendant conjecture, error and embellishment. The spread of the potato is also the stuff of legend. It is not just the story of the struggle to combat famine in the West, spearheaded by 18th-century *laissez-faire* advocates but an appalling fact for the Irish population in the mid-19th century.

Potato

The potato spread to the four corners of the world with astonishing success. Its role for the future will be crucial wherever hunger rears its head, but it also has its place in a balanced diet for over-fed societies. This book celebrates the potato's progress, and pays homage to a vegetable that is neither old fashioned nor Euro-centric.

The potato might be said to have enjoyed its golden age in the 19th century, when good plain cooks were producing classics such as Leek and Potato Soup, Cottage Pie and Duchesse Potatoes. These are delicious recipes, but the grand works of hearty gastronomy from that period already do the potato proud, and there are plenty of recipe books in the same vein to cater to regressive tastes. The recipes described here are indebted to those classics. However, the focus of this book is the meeting of an international potato with the chefs of the world. It therefore necessarily reflects contemporary cooking. It is not written in praise of fusion cuisine, rather it puts the case for *dif*fusion cuisine. The potato is universal and belongs to everyone.

The potato has been travelling for five centuries. It is the wish of all those who have contributed to this book to accompany it part of the way.

The Potato: Splendour and Misery

The Potato: Splendour and Misery

Because it has a high nutritional value and is easy to cultivate, the potato can provide a lot of people with a complete food from very few resources. Its domestication in the Andes, where its story began, goes back thousands of years.

All Andean civilisations adopted the potato. It features in their mythologies and symbolic representations of a world in which man depends on nature. These complex civilisations, famous for their incredible feats of engineering, depended on a numerous and obedient population who were hungry for work and fed on potatoes. The Inca Empire of the 16th century is the ultimate example.

The Spanish discovered the Inca Empire while searching for gold and new territories for their own empire, and they applied what they learned from the Incas to their colonial politics and defence of the Catholic faith in Europe. The Spanish Golden Age, which reached its peak under Philip II, was a time of religious wars in which the Andean potato played a strategic role.

In the Andes, the importance of the potato was plain for all to see: there was never any secret made of it. When the Spanish adopted it, they deliberately cloaked it in mystery and subjected it to a law of silence. No trace of its voyage across the Atlantic can be found in the plethora of inventories listing cargo from 'New Spain'. Nor was there any mention of it by botanists working on Spanish soil, although the new interest in the sciences during the Renaissance and the introduction of hitherto unknown plants made this group of people very active. It was only in the 20th century that research brought to light a couple of chance references to the potato. They occur in two loading accounts dating from the second half of the 16th century from the Canary Isles, and in accounts showing purchases of potatoes by a charitable institution in Seville, written up at the same time. Clearly, Spain involved the potato in its holy war in Europe.

Preceding pages: around Cuzco in Peru, 'chicha' or maize beer is poured over the potatoes as an offering before planting

The progress of the potato escaped this Spanish embargo however and spread to the rest of Europe. The first scholarly writings on the tuber date from the beginning of the 18th century. Yet people still kept quiet about it and grew it out of sight behind walls, particularly to avoid the taxman's eagle eye. But its benefits were already starting to take effect on European demography. Scurvy disappeared along with other vitamin deficiency related illnesses and the population increased. In Ireland, where the population was decimated after a period of continual war, its effect was remarkable. The agrarian revolution at the end of the century put the potato in the fields and brought it firmly to the fore in agriculture and crop-growing.

In the 19th century, its development took a dramatic downturn. In Ireland, the socio-political context imposed by Protestant England resulted in agricultural workers and Catholics subsisting entirely on potatoes. Hundreds of thousands of men and women died and millions left the country forever in the wake of a potato blight that ravaged the crops.

The potato, however, has remained a unique source of significant advantages: it has high nutritional content and needs minimal resources for cultivation and consumption. This is its strength, but also its weakness when it falls under oppressive regimes. Although it has released people from hunger, it relies on legislation to emancipate it.

Some examples of edible Andean plants

Left: On the banks of the River Llave in Peru, an Aimara woman prepares potatoes for 'chuño' (see inset p. 16)

The Andean potato: secret wealth

For thousands of years, probably since the Neolithic Age and well before the successive waves of the great Pre-Colombian civilisations, Andean farmers were working with nature and honing their relations with her. The remains of cults practising before the Spanish Conquest give evidence of this. The potato was quick to become part of the South American diet. The oldest traces go back 13,000 years. They come from archaeological excavations in the centre of southern Chile and show that the wild potato was being gathered there.

Potatoes have been grown in Peru for at least 8,000 years. Andean farmers worked the natural environment so efficiently that they hold the record for the number of edible species of roots and tubers they brought under cultivation, of which the potato, with eight cultivated species is merely the most famous. They are grown on smallholdings on the Altiplano, or high plain, a vast area located at over 4,000 metres above sea level with mountain peaks all around rising to over 6,000m.

In the Tropics, the mountain ranges are associated with a wide variety of microclimates. A day's walking in the Andes can take you from temperate valleys up to the cold, arid and windy heights of the Altiplano. Alternatively, you can go down from the temperate zones to wet, low-level, tropical regions. To benefit from the different climatic regions, Andean farmers soon diversified their crops. Along the 4,000km-long chain of mountains, at altitudes similar to the more

'Solanum Yungasense', a wild species

clement regions of Piedmont, these farmers (or rather gardeners: they worked with spades and had no animals or ploughs) domesticated more edible plants than any other continent. At high altitudes in an extreme landscape, on terraces clinging to the precipitous slopes of the Cordillera, the potato began its life as a domesticated plant and became the staple diet for Andean civilisations.

Before Spanish colonisation, every stone that supports these terraced fields was laid without the aid of iron tools. The earth was brought up on men's shoulders and turned using the *chaki taqlla*, a kind of spade with a foot rest suitable for major levelling; it is still used today by Andean farmers. Crop rotation, soil quality (often poor in the mountains) and the varying sorts of crop that could be grown in the different microclimates soon led to farms being divided into parcels, an agrarian system that persists in the Andes.

Potato field near Lake Umayo, in Peru

Left: Terraced fields in the Andes

Genetic diversity

Wild species of potato, which have very small tubers, grow in all sorts of soils and climates, from the dry deserts beside the Pacific to Andean valleys at 2,500 to 3,200 metres above sea level. A few species grow at extreme altitudes, like the *Solanum acaule*, a frost-resistant variety, while others grow in wet, tropical zones around the Amazonian basin, like the *Solanum urubambae* and *Solanum yungasense*.

The cultivated types have adapted to less extreme conditions, but many still prefer cold climes, wind and well-drained sites to produce a successful crop. They are grown from wild species by cross-cultivation and selection, and are therefore both the fruits of chance and expert choice. The eight domesticated types in the Andes, *Solanum stenotomum*, *Solanum goniocalyx*, *Solanum phureja*, *Solanum tuberosum* subspecies *andigena* (an ancestor of the potato we know today worldwide), *Solanum x chaucha*, *Solanum ajanhuiri*, *Solanum juzepczukii*, and *Solanum hygrothermicum* have produced thousands of cultivars (see inset, p14). (A cultivar is a new choice of plant developed from a cultivated species for one or more naturally occurring features.)

Andean farmers can grow between 2 and 50 different potatoes on a one-hectare parcel. Their yields are poor. These 'heritage' varieties, called 'gift potatoes', are rarely sold. They are given to prestigious guests and used in special dishes at ceremonial dinners, when the broad range of shape, taste and colour is seen as a sign of gastronomic know-how and promotes lively conversation. Indeed, the traditional cultivars bear

The Andean Potatoes

Solanum stenotomum

Called **pitiquiña** *and thought to be the earliest of the domesticated potatoes,* **Solanum stenotomum** *produces long, cylindrical, bumpy, sometimes spiralling tubers that can be red, black or white. It has a nutty flavour and high levels of protein and Vitamin C. It is becoming rarer and is only grown in the Andes. Some forms are frost-resistant, and the tubers need to go through a dormant phase to germinate.*

Solanum goniocalyx

Called **limeña** *in the Andes or* **papa amarilla** *('yellow potato'),* **Solanum goniocalyx** *is an exceptionally tasty, dark yellow potato. It is fried and sold on the streets of Lima and is popular in Peruvian cooking. Very like the* **pitiquiña** *and possibly a subspecies, it grows in the temperate regions of the Andes. It is widely grown for its much-loved culinary properties and flavour.*

Solanum phureja

The **phureja** *is a small, irregular-shaped potato with a very fine flavour. It is grown at lower levels (2,200 to 2,600m) than other species on the warm, wet, east-facing slopes of the Andes from Venezuela to northern Argentina. It is little known outside the Andes, except in Holland where it is recognised for its resistance to disease. It is suitable for high temperatures and has been a gene-provider to two of the most heat-resistant varieties of European potato. It has no dormancy period, which is an advantage because it can produce several harvests a year, but a disadvantage when it comes to selling it.*

Solanum tuberosum *subspecies* andigena

The **andigena** *is the ancestor of the European potato. Although botanically very close, it bears no physical resemblance. Probably the most farmed Andean potato, it grows just as well on mountainsides in Mexico and Central America as along the Cordillera, from Venezuela to Argentina. Its tubers are the biggest of all the traditional potatoes. However it is sensitive to attacks of* **Phytophthora infestans** *and is often under-productive, although certain varieties give yields of 30 tonnes per hectare (the average yield of the ordinary potato is 16 tonnes per hectare). With over 3,000 cultivars, the* **andigena** *boasts more varieties than any other Andean potato.*

Solanum x chaucha

The cultivated type is called the **huayro** *and is a hybrid of the* **Solanum stenotomum** *and* **Solanum tuberosum** *subsp.* **andigena**. *The plant starts early in the season and the tubers need no dormancy period. It is very widely farmed from Colombia to north-west Argentina and is one of the most commercialised potatoes among the Indian population. In Peru, it has spread from the Altiplano to virtually the entire country and its future looks bright. The tubers are far larger than those of the traditional varieties, probably on account of it starting out as a hybrid.*

Solanum ajanhuiri

The **ajanhuiri** *is a very hardy species, in other words it is very frost-resistant. It is widely grown at altitudes of 3,800 to 4,000m on the Altiplano in the area around Lake Titicaca to the south of Peru and north-west Bolivia. In a hostile environment where frost places serious constraints on agricultural development, only a few species of plant can be farmed. It contains high levels of dry matter and vitamin C and is an excellent keeper. Only the clone* **sisu** *can be eaten without preparation. The other types are bitter and turned into chuño, a freeze-dried potato. The* **ajanhuiri** *matures early and can resist temperatures as low as -5°C, as well as hail, drought and viral diseases. Although recognised by the scientific and horticultural world for some 50 years, it is little used in selection projects for new varieties. Despite photoperiodic constraints (see inset p17) at temperate latitudes (not an insuperable constraint), the* **ajanhuiri** *is a potato with a promising future.*

Solanum x juzepczukii *and* Solanum x curtilobum

The **rucki** *potato, developed from two hybrid species, is probably the most frost-resistant of the domesticated potatoes. It grows in central and southern Peru and northern Bolivia at altitudes as high as 4,200m. At this height, it is often subjected to frost while it is growing. Both species come from cross-fertilizations between a wild and a domesticated species that occur at the edge of the fields. Both also contain genes from* **Solanum acaule**, *a tiny wild species that grows very high up at the limits of the everlasting snows. They have been cultivated since well before the Incas and are still grown despite poor yields - between 2.5 and 5 tonnes per hectare. Neither has been the object of agricultural improvement. They provide constant food in a region where frosts can occur 300 days a year. Their tubers are bitter and can only be eaten after being treated. They are used for making chuño.*

Solanum hygrothermicum

This is the only species that is happy in a semi-tropical region with 2,000 to 3,000mm of rainfall a year. Its advantages as a hot-climate potato and a source of genes for varieties that can grow in high temperatures is significant today, because it is very rare and probably on the verge of extinction.

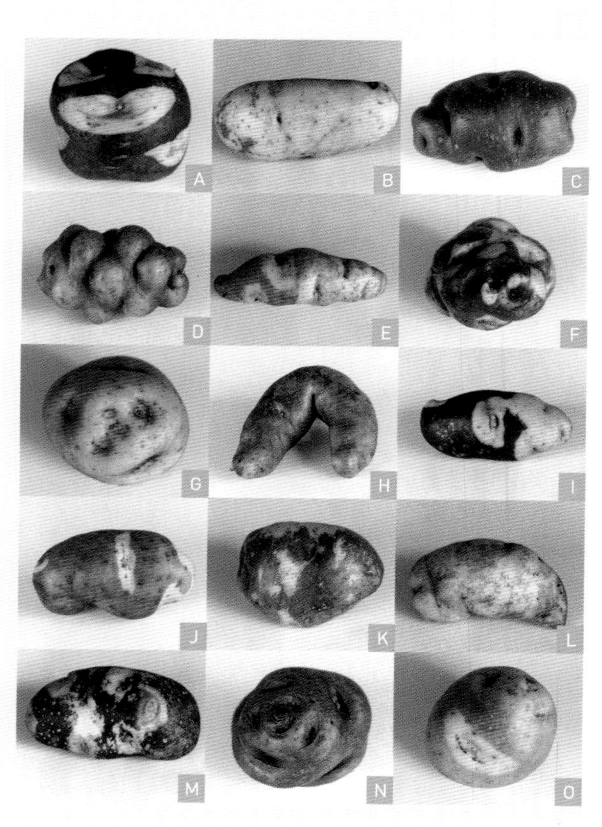

The vernacular names of the Andean cultivars are in quechua or aimara.

A Kuntur warmi: 'like a woman with the colours of the condor's neck'
B Waka qallu: 'as fat as a cow's tongue'
C Yana wayru: 'the most beautiful of the dark women'
D Llunchuy waqachi: 'makes the daughter-in-law cry'
E Wara suru: 'shepherd's crook'
F Santo Domingo: 'like Saint Domingo's clothes'
G Kumpis: 'a fine potato'
H Puka suyt'u: 'red and long'
I Quwi obispo: 'like a guinea pig with fur the colour of a bishop's gown'
J Quwi sullu: 'guinea pig's foetus'
K Yana calabaza: 'black pumpkin'
L Puka pepino: 'red cucumber'
M Cheqche suytu: 'long and speckled'
N Doce colores: 'three-coloured flesh'
O Allqa rihra: 'like a two-coloured shoulder'

humorous names, such as 'makes the daughter-in-law cry' or 'like an old bone' (see plate p14). In areas where the labour market is tight, they can also be used to attract agricultural workers who are paid in kind.

On the farms, it is the women who are responsible for gathering these traditional varieties; they know the names and oversee the 'seed potatoes', the tubers that are planted. The men leave it to the women to name them, and the women are also in charge of selling them in the markets.

Feeding the masses in Andean civilisations

When the conquistadores took possession of the Inca Empire, they discovered a strongly hierarchical civilisation centred on the Andes and settled in the area stretching from today's border between Ecuador and Colombia to the River Maule in Chile. The Incas knew how to exploit the complementarity of their coastal and mountain regions. They had developed an irrigation system by building aqueducts to bring mountain water to the fields on the dry plains bordering the Pacific. Major road builders, they had constructed a network of paved carriageways linking the four corners of the Empire to transport a compost of seabird droppings to the high, infertile lands where the potato was grown, and to promote exchange between regions.

The Pre-Inca civilisations already understood the advantages of their geographic position. Potatoes cultivated in the Sierra fed not only the mountain farmers but also the population living beside the ocean. The potato and the chuño (see inset p16), brought by herds of llamas from the mountains to the coast, had fed the coastal inhabitants since time immemorial. The chronicler Pedro Cieza de León (c.1520-1554) described potatoes growing near the coast in the semi-desert valleys and dependent on irrigation. At the time of the Conquest, therefore, Pre-Colombian farmers were already able to grow varieties that were suited to heat, but they had vanished without trace by the 18th century.

Archaeological excavations of Pre-Colombian tombs along the coast have brought to light numerous examples of chuño in the graves. Pre-Inca pottery, like that of the Mochicas along the north coast of Peru or the Nazcas in the south, proves that the potato and the chuño played a crucial role in the lives of these people since the earliest times. The potato was used as a unit of measurement in both time and space. The time it took to cook a pot of potatoes was a unit of time, while the surface area necessary to grow a year's supply of potatoes for a family was called a *papacancha*, from the word *papa* meaning 'potato' in Quechua, the Inca language. In Spanish-speaking countries in South America, the potato is still called *papa*. It has enabled peoples to inhabit the high plateaux; without it, Peruvian civilisations would never have reached such a level of complexity.

The Inca Empire was based on a policy of military conquest that procured local riches for the Inca, the supreme authority, and for the Incas, the aristocratic and religious apparatus that governed a mosaic of peoples. With no money to speak of, the Incas had established a

'Chuño negro' and 'chuño blanco' (see inset, following page)

barter economy based on the exchange of goods and people. This enabled them to levy three types of tax in kind: the tribute, movement of people and compulsory labour. The Empire of the 'children of the Sun' depended on an obedient population that lived under the military and religious rule of the Inca authority. On the eve of the Spanish conquest, the Inca population was about ten million strong.

Every time a new territory was conquered, people were moved about for the benefit of the rulers. Communities arrived who were completely loyal to the Inca and new subjects departed for the Empire's most faithful lands. The *mita* was a form of taxation based on compulsory labour and consisting of service of public works for military purposes. It could include heavy and complex hydraulic work, building roads and magnificent imperial edifices and working in artisanal workshops.

Everything required for these tasks, as well as the tribute and the *mitayos*, or those called to the *mita*, demanded efficient means of transport and stop-overs and came under centralised control. To this end, a network of roads divided up the Andes with inns and warehouses along the way. Textiles and potatoes, pottery and tools, armies and administrators, *mitayos* and deported peoples all passed through. With its all-powerful economy and communications, this highly organised system that depended on strength was able to devote a major share of its resources to taxation and its administration.

Inca farming, with its two basic staples (maize, cultivated between 1,500 and 3,500m, and the potato cultivated up to 4,200m), was entirely controlled by the Empire. A third of the harvests went to the Inca storehouses, a third to the clergy and a third to the community. Maize and potatoes produced high yields proportional to the land and time needed to farm them. Consequently there was no shortage of people available to work for the tribute and the *mita*. Maize was reserved almost exclusively for the upper echelons of society, while potatoes were fed to the community and could be stored as chuño for long periods.

Reserve food: the chuño

The reserve food farmed on the high Andean plateaux is the chuño, *a freeze-dried potato. It can be prepared in two ways, called white chuño and black chuño. The potatoes are first sorted according to size. For white chuño, the tubers are left out in the frost over night then sun-dried during the day, and after several days of this treatment, they are trampled under foot to get rid of the water and skins and to flatten them. This process is followed by thirty days in running water to eliminate poisons in them that are not destroyed by cooking and which can give them a bitter taste.* Rucki *potatoes contain a high percentage of these substances so the rinsing stage is essential. Then they are again dried in the sun and a white deposit forms on the surface.*
The preparation of chuño negro *is almost identical but the skin is left on. There is no washing and the chuño turns very dark brown, hence its name. It is soaked in water for a day or two before cooking to get rid of any bitterness.*
The chuño is very light and easy to transport. It is simply soaked in water before cooking. It is not harmed by frost and can be kept for several years.
When the potato is cooked in water, peeled and cut into strips then sun-dried and finely milled, it becomes papa seca, *or dry potato. This is popular in the cities especially in Peru and forms the basis of a dish called* carapulcra *made of meat, tomatoes, onions and garlic.*
The table below (from J.A. Wolfe, The Potato in the Human Diet*) shows the comparative nutritional values for 100g of raw potatoes, both types of* chuño *and dry potato. Note the massive increase in energy values, due to their concentration, in the* chuño *and* papa seca, *as well as the high levels of carbohydrates, calcium, phosphorus and iron, and in the* chuño negro *and* papa seca, *concentrations of protein. Vitamin C levels show a dramatic drop, however.*

Product	Energy (mg)	Protein (g)	Carbohydrate (g)	Calcium (mg)	Potassium (mg)	Iron (mg)	Vitamin B1 (mg)	Vitamin B2 (mg)	Vitamin PP (mg)	Vitamin C (mg)
Potato	1 335	2.1	18.5	09	050	0.8	0.10	0.04	1.50	20
Chuño blanco	1 351	1.9	77.5	92	054	3.3	0.03	0.04	0.38	1.1
Chuño negro	1 393	4.0	79.4	44	203	0.9	0.13	0.17	3.40	1.7
Papa seca	1 347	8.2	72.6	47	200	4.5	0.19	0.09	05.0	3.2

The potato and above all the chuño, which was always available, travelled well and contained concentrated nutritional values which were vital to the Incas to feed 'that most precious wealth: the arms and energy of their peoples' (Alfred Métraux[1]), who were serving the Empire and constantly on the move. An endless stream of Inca armies, displaced peoples and men and their families who were called to the *mita* passed along the Empire's roads, and the Inca fed them on these journeys and during their public or military service.

The Inca Empire was entirely ignorant of the rest of the world including their Meso-American neighbours, and it was completely taken by surprise when the conquerors from the Old World arrived.

The Spanish landed in Peru in 1532 while searching for gold and spreading the Catholic faith. They were genuinely astonished by the complexity and efficiency of the Inca Empire, then at the pinnacle of its success. And they soon realised the value of the potato in this civilisation.

The potato in the golden age

When the potato arrived in Europe in the 16th century after the Spanish conquest of the Inca Empire (1532-1570), European farmers were quick to tackle the constraints of photoperiodism (see inset). Cultivars suited to the new conditions of growth were selected from *Solanum tuberosum* subsp. *andigena*, the form introduced. The first successful potato crops were grown in areas of Europe where frosts arrive very late. This meant that the potatoes from *andigena* plants could finish growing without risk of being killed by frost.

This was the case in southern Spain. The accounts of the hospital of La Sangre y Las Cinco Llagas in Seville (built in 1546) show that from 1573 potatoes were bought during the winter months, mostly in December and January and sometimes in November and February. These were locally harvested potatoes that had tuberised late (i.e., ready for lifting at the end of the year) and were clearly of Andean origin and had not yet acclimatised. The purchases listed are not numerous; however from 1576 they increased, and from 1580, were substantial. This leads one to suppose that the hospital was inspired to make more purchases because prices had fallen and the market was already flourishing.

1. For quoted works, see bibliography, p.190.

The 'pachamanca' or underground oven made of hot stones, used throughout the Andes

Page16 Chuño in the market in Pisac, Peru

Photoperiodism

Potato tubers form in response to the number of daylight hours. This is called photoperiodism. In tropical latitudes between 23° N and 23° S, which is the cradle of the potato, the tubers grow when days and nights are of equal length. On the other hand in mid latitudes between 30° and 50° N, where climates are temperate and summer days are long, as in the case of Europe, potatoes need to acclimatise for tuberisation to occur. Otherwise it happens at the Autumn equinox when days and nights are both 12 hours' long, as in the tropics, but when temperatures are falling and frosts are possible. Without heat and sun, tubers are few and very small.
This problem can be solved if tubers from plants that produce the biggest tubers are chosen for replanting year after year. Today, the potato plants selected grow in any latitude.

San Diego feeds the poor in Seville with a cauldron of potatoes (painting by E. Murillo, 1645)

Religious conflict, Spanish grandeur and Peruvian silver

The 16th century in Europe was one of religious conflict that set Catholics against Protestants. Catholic Spain was the most powerful kingdom in the continent (see map p.25), and its kings were on a religious mission to put down the rise of Protestantism on Spanish soil. Philip II (1556-1598) led a bloody repression of Holland, which had been under Spanish rule since 1516 and where the impact of the Reform was a threat to the stability of the Empire. In 1567 he dispatched his armies, and in 1578 his nephew and most brilliant strategist, Alexander Farnese, Duke of Parma and Piacenza, took control of the country. Italy was then ruled by his uncle, the most powerful prince of the peninsula. In some areas, the potato grew so abundantly that it was used to feed pigs. The Dutch repression was a costly business for the Crown, and Philip II found the silver from his Peruvian colony a useful source of revenue with which to finance his wars. Indeed the silver, which was appearing in hitherto unheard-of quantities and being circulated throughout Europe, completely transformed the economy. Two Spanish ports played a crucial role in this transformation, Seville and Antwerp.

Seville at that time was hugely rich, and with 150,000 inhabitants in 1590, was one of the most highly populated cities in the West. It had the monopoly on

After extraction from the Cerro Rico, silver was mixed with mercury in paved enclosures and trampled under foot by the Indians in Potosí (late 16th century)

trade with Spanish territories in the New World, which represented a truly fairy-tale market. Everything with which Europe could provide its colonies set sail from the port of Seville. The 'American treasure' - the silver ingots that had travelled from the heart of the Andes to Seville - was the merchandise that made the city glorious. A fifth of the treasure was kept by the King. Seville was also home to the biggest scientific community in Spain and was the capital of Spanish printing. The study of American flora and its impact on medicine feature among the first subjects of research. The high point of the yearly calendar of exchange between Seville and Transatlantic Spain was the arrival of the ships from the

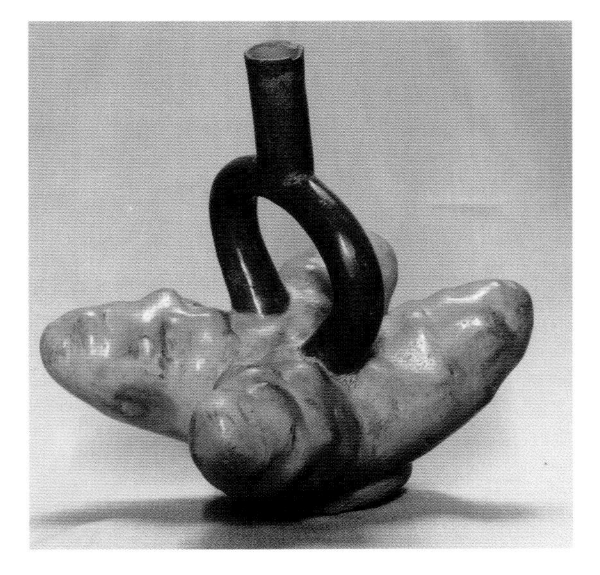

Three pottery items from the Mochica civilisation (200BC-700AD), from left to right: 'potato twins', from the Huayro cultivar; anthropomorphic potato vessel in an attitude of reverence, and vessel made of tubers with a human face

Francisco Pisarro (1475-1541),
conqueror of the Inca Empire

A glimpse of the range of potatoes sold in the market in Pisac, Peru

Indies, as the Americas were then called, carrying with them white metal and placed under good escort. Year after year, a magnificent procession of eight galleons of war made its way up the Guadalquivir, laden with a cargo that made the whole of Europe dream of trade and finance and which was awaited impatiently by bankers and merchants. Between 1503 and 1600, 7,593 tonnes of precious metal, of which only 2% was gold, officially arrived from the mines of Potosí, then in Peru and today in Bolivia, a town entirely built by the Spanish in 1545 and perched at 4,000m above sea level.

Antwerp was the other great port for maritime trade with the Spanish colonies. An international centre of exchange it was central to the network of cities that controlled trade and finance, a network dominated by Genoan and Flemish merchants. Cargos from Seville were channelled through this

Nazca pottery, a Pre-Inca culture (200BC-600AD), showing an anthropomorphic potato

network to finance war and trade in Europe and the East. Letters of exchange could be used for European trade, but trade in luxury goods with the East (spices, silk and precious wood) required hard currency, and it was silver, overvalued in Eastern economies, that was demanded in payment. The Spanish piece of eight, a silver coin, was currency not only throughout Europe but throughout the whole of Asia.

Financing the war was therefore assured by the flow of Peruvian silver, but the Crown still needed to feed its troops without resorting to pillage. The scandalous sack of Rome, perpetrated by German mercenaries in the Spanish army in 1527, had seriously tarnished the image of Spain in Europe.

Feeding the masses in the Spanish Empire

The Spanish were not slow to spot the role the potato had played in the Inca Empire. They had noticed that this huge population who laboured for the state were healthy and vigorous and that they lived almost exclusively on this crop. They therefore adopted the same system in the extraction of Peruvian silver.

When they arrived in South America, the Spanish were convinced that they were going to find gold. The myth of Eldorado that inspired the conquistadores placed the Chibcha area at the heart of this legendary land. The Spanish realised that this was where the finest gold objects came from, and in 1537 they sent Jiménez de Quesada (1509-1579) to prospect. The first encounter with the potato appears in the record of this expedition. Quesada, a cultivated military man posted to Santa Marta on the Caribbean coast of what is today Colombia, was instructed to travel up the River Magdalena to its source in the hopes of reaching the Chibcha plateau that fed it.

Only a third of the expedition survived the ascent of the Cordillera, an area covered in swampy jungle. Worn out, sick and above all famished after days spent living off boiled leather from their equipment, then off meat from their dead companions, they finally reached the plateau. The region was rich and densely populated, with booty for the taking. The welcome they received was warm; nevertheless, Quesada's men threw themselves into wanton pillage. One of them wrote an account of the business, although his report remained unpublished until 1886. The Spanish forced their way into people's houses and found maize, beans and what they took for 'truffles' but which were in fact potatoes. The account also described plants 'with full, purple flowers and floury roots that have a good flavour, are offered as gifts by the Indians and which represent a refined dish even for the Spanish'. Quesada himself noticed the vast harvests these truffles produced.

Another encounter between the Spanish and the potato took place in Colombia a few months later in 1538. The chronicler Pedro Cieza de León, who wrote at night after days spent on the march, described it in his book published

Convoy of llamas laden with silver ingots from the Potosí mines (engraving by Théodore de Bry, 1528-1598, published in 'Americae' in 1602)

in 1550, *The War of Quito*. In his next book, *Chronicles of Peru*, published three years later in 1553, he expressed his bitterness at the Spanish who had made massive profits by shamelessly selling chuño at outrageous prices to Indian *mitayos* in the Potosí silver mines, having bought it for next to nothing from the farmers. José de Acosta, a Jesuit and defender of the Indians, noted in his book *Natural History of the Indies* published in 1590, that in the lands around Cuzco, the capital of the Inca Empire, the potato was the staple diet and that there was a major trade in chuño to the Potosí silver mines. Gold, however, there was none. Eldorado, 'the man of gold', turned out to be a 'silver mountain'.

In 1545, the Spanish learned that there was a seam of silver in the mountains at over 4,000m in a lunar landscape to the south of Lake Titicaca where all agriculture was impossible. They built the town of Potosí from the ground up for the purpose of mining the Cerro Rico, the 'silver mountain'. Potosí became one of the most highly populated cities in the world in the 16th century, with 120,000 inhabitants in 1572 and 160,000 in 1650 when it began to decline. The Spanish were quick to adopt the system of the *mita* (mentioned earlier) - compulsory service and the displacement of populations - to be sure of Indian labour to work the mine and transport precious metals to the coast, from where it was shipped to the Isthmus of Panama. In Potosí, food had to be carried by convoys of llamas and mules, which meant constant food stops, and the miners had to be fed as cheaply as possible.

The Spanish merchants therefore quickly established a trade in chuño, selling it at a price the Indians could only afford by going into debt. Food, the cost of candles for lighting the mine and tools were all sold at exorbitant prices. Compulsory service, or fixed-term slavery, was prolonged by debt to force the exhausted miners, who had nothing to call their own and suffered by turn the extreme heat of the mine then the glacial chill of nights at the surface of the Altiplano, to spend the rest of their lives working for the merchants. Unable to pay off their fathers' debts, the miners' children could do nothing but follow in their footsteps.

In 1572 when mercury was discovered and the Huancavelica mercury mines in Peru were opened, mining intensified. Mining-related diseases (tuberculosis and silicosis) now included mercury poisoning. Moreover, the Indians had to tread the amalgam under foot in an ironic echo of making chuño, which was almost entirely responsible for keeping them alive. Thousands of men died each year and Potosí was nicknamed the 'jaws of hell'.

Forty years passed between the discovery of the Inca Empire and the beginning of silver mining in Potosí. From the outset of the conquest, the Spanish both adopted the Incas' system of compulsory service and commandeered the potato, feeding it to Spanish troops who were fighting to uphold Catholicism. Immediately, they treated the potato as a military secret. And it was not long before they had acclimatised the tuber for themselves.

So it was that in 1567, the potato was said to be growing in the Spanish Canaries. We know from documentary sources that before the end of the 16th century, the potato was cultivated and sold in Seville and that it was widely grown in Italy. On the other hand, no scientific work makes reference to it. Neither Spanish botanists nor their Italian counterparts published a single line on the potato. Had the Spanish state decided to subject all information on the potato to military censorship?

Spanish and Italian Omerta: a very Catholic silence

Only recently (1992) have the vagaries of research uncovered entries of the potato in lawyers' loading books on the Canary Islands. Dated 28 November 1567, a certain Juan de la Molina dispatched three barrels from Las Palmas in Gran Canaria containing potatoes, oranges and limes to his brother Luis de Quesada in Antwerp, so right to the heart of the Protestant dispute on Spanish territory. Another lawyer recorded a load of two barrels of potatoes and eight of Cognac from Tenerife, still in Juan de la Molina's name and dated 24 April 1574, this time destined for the port of Rouen in France. Rouen was at the height of its trade and, like Antwerp, was home to an active Protestant population. Both cities were important in the spread of Protestant Humanism owing to their printing workshops.

At that time, the Canary Islands were used for acclimatising plants from sub-tropical zones in the Old World, which were bound for plantations in the New World. The same was true of plants travelling in the opposite direction. Business was booming and a large colony of Genoan and Flemish merchants had settled in the Canaries. Potatoes could be cultivated at this latitude (40°N), where winters were very mild and made two harvests possible, one at the end of autumn, the other in spring, as the two dates in the account books suggest. Some thirty years after Francisco Pisarro arrived in Peru in 1531, the potato was being grown on Spanish soil in southern Europe.

The potatoes dispatched to Antwerp by Juan de la Molina seem to have disappeared into thin air. There is no trace of later dispatches that would indicate efforts to start a European trade in potatoes, as happened with sugar from the Canaries.

The most famous Spanish botanist, Sévillan Nicolas Monardes (1493-1588), a doctor from Genoa who collected plants from the New World and grew them in his own private garden in the city, published nothing on the potato. Yet he was the author of descriptions of tobacco, sunflowers and peanuts, all plants from the New World.

The potato and perfidious Albion

English botanists did not show the same knowledge and expertise in potato growing as their continental colleagues. The botanical descriptions in their books were fanciful and smacked of patriotism. Indeed, they seemed to want to prove that the potato did not come from Spanish territory - Spain was a Catholic power and a sworn enemy, especially after 1588 and the defeat of the Spanish Armada - but from English domains in the New World, particularly Virginia founded by Sir Walter Raleigh in 1584 and named in honour of Elizabeth I (1533-1603), the Virgin Queen.
John Gerard, who published a work on the potato in 1597, is most to blame for the confusion surrounding its origins. He was gardener to Lord Burghley, the most powerful man in England, Minister of Finance and the Queen's closest adviser. According to Gerard, it was the sweet potato that came from Peru. The conquistadores' chronicles were never cited. In England, a knowing confusion was created around the words papa *and* batatta, *the name of the sweet potato in Arawak, an Indian language of the Meso-American region spoken in the Caribbean at the time of the Spanish conquest. It was in the Caribbean that English buccaneers put Spanish galleons to rout. Did they receive wrong information and thus confuse the two plants? The sweet potato grows in hot tropical zones and, again for reasons of photoperiodism, cannot grow in summer north of a latitude of 40° without acclimatisation. This combined with the potato's need for warmth means that it can grow in the south of Spain. Today, the English potato and the word used in Castilian Spanish,* patata, *are an echo of this confusion.*
Clusius (see the section on Botanic Progress by the Protestants, *p26), who made several visits to England during the 1570s and translated Thomas Harriot's* Brief and True Report of the Newfoundland of Virginia, *merely acknowledged that there were similarities between the potato of Virginia and the* papa, *and he did not cite any English authors in his works. Gaspard Bauhin, in his* Prodromos Theatri Botanici *of 1616, assumed that the potato had come from Virginia. Jean Bauhin, his elder brother, followed suit and quoted Harriot's work in a posthumous book not published till 1651. He also referred to the Peruvian* papa *and quoted the conquistadores' works.*

View of Antwerp (engraving of 1549)

Another prominent figure in contemporary Sevillian medicine was Simon de Tovar. He too kept a botanical garden, but he published nothing on the potato. Yet he produced annual catalogues about plants and corresponded with his peers all over Europe.

The only works to appear in Spain at this period in which the potato gets a mention were the accounts of the first chroniclers in the New World. Many of them were never printed, and many were only translated much later in the 19th-century craze for English versions. Royal censorship was imposed on all publications about Spanish possessions in the New World. Moreover, in a Europe where the language of scholarly literature was Latin, these Spanish-language chronicles could only be distributed confidentially.

Italy, where the potato was widespread, was home to some of the most prestigious botanical gardens in Europe, including the oldest in Padua where botanists studied the latest plants to arrive in the Old World. Pierandrea Mattioli, known as Matthiolus (1501-1577), whose fame equalled that of Monardes in Spain, wrote a description of the tomato, which had arrived from the New World shortly before the potato. There can be no doubting his interest in New World plants, yet he wrote nothing about the potato. Thus, within one of the most active scholarly societies of the time, the potato was not yet recognised.

In southern Europe, the two Spanish territories where the potato grew and where a major community of botanists was working seem to have been subjected to the same censorship.

The potato and the Spanish war effort

After the conquest in the Andes, the potato held no more secrets for the Spanish. With it in their possession, growing in areas of their empire where climatic conditions meant that photoperiodism was not too much of a problem, and fully aware of how to cultivate it, they were now in a position to make it part of their troops' diet. In addition, the size of the fleet in the Mediterranean, which requisitioned Sicilian wheat for ships' biscuits, must have prompted military suppliers to resort to the potato.

Spanish troops and mercantile and financial traffic all used the same south-north corridor to cross Europe (see map opposite). The famous Italian *tercios*, or elite soldiers, and mercenaries like the German Landsknecht, marched along it on their way to the Low Countries. Heavily protected gold for wages, which Genoan merchants had collected from every small lender in Europe, also travelled this route, to be exchanged for white Spanish metal when the fleet from the Indies landed in Seville.

One would think that, in the convoys that furnished the Spanish armies and their demanding supply corps, and in the luggage of the thousands of Spanish and Italian merchants who used these prosperous roads, the potato had ample opportunity for travel. It provided troops with a complete diet and made them less likely to steal food as the Spanish crown feared. All this would suggest that Spain in the 16th century had established a sort of ring of silence around the potato in order to keep an easily prepared, high-energy and profitable food for its own war effort.

It was not until the beginning of the 17th century in 1601 that the first publication on the potato appeared in Spanish lands. The work of a Protestant, it was published by the famous Plantin printing house in Antwerp (see p26). But by now the secret was already out. As it moved around with the Spanish armies, the potato had already spread across Europe. Could it be that in sending potatoes from the Canaries to Antwerp, Juan de la Molina had endeavoured to provide the Protestants of northern Europe with the means to conduct experiments?

Botanical progress by Protestant scholars

The first work to deal with potato growing in Europe was *Théâtre d'agriculture et mesnage des champs (Theatre of Agriculture and Care of Fields)* published in 1600. Its author, Olivier de Serres (1539-1619), was a Protestant gentleman living on his lands in the Vivarais area in France. Although he claimed only to have just learnt of the potato, he knew all about growing it and deciding what soil and feed would suit it best, as well as about 'banking up', an essential stage that involves covering the above-ground stems to encourage growth of the tubers and plentiful harvests. He also

GEOPOLITICAL MAP OF THE POTATO IN THE 16TH CENTURY

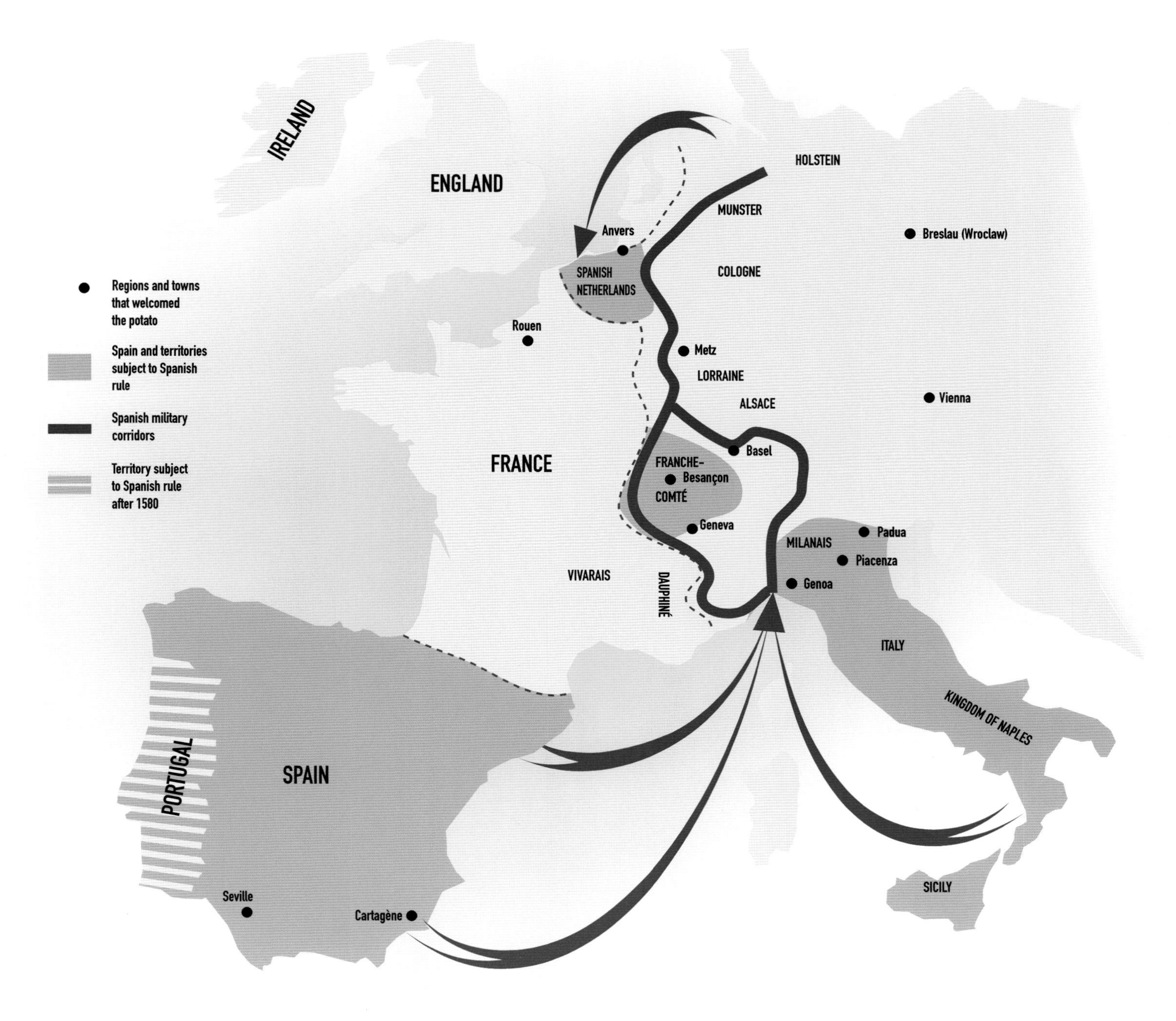

This map shows the war effort of the Spanish armies who relied on Sicily, the Kingdom of Naples, the Milanais, the Franche-Comté, the Spanish Netherlands and the good will of German principalities (see F. Braudel, 'Material Civilization, Economy and Capitalism'). (NB: we have added the names of places that welcomed the potato in the 16th century and which are mentioned in the text.)

indicated that he had received potatoes from Switzerland, then from the Dauphiné. Switzerland and the Dauphiné were for the most part Protestant, and the Spanish military routes skirted these regions (see map). Olivier de Serres wrote: 'One banks up the branches with all the stems as many times as possible until August.' *His* potatoes were ripe 'at the end of September'. The problem of photoperiodism seems therefore to have been completely solved for plants from southern Europe. It had taken less than 27 years to bring harvests forward by two months, for in 1573, *andigena* potatoes had been lifted in November in Seville. This shows that potatoes grown in Italy for Spanish armies had been perfectly acclimatised.

The name Olivier de Serres gave these potatoes was 'cartouffles'. Although they were described in the section about ornamental plants suitable for winter gardens, arbours, bowers and the like - where, among other things, de Serres described the tomato - he gave perfectly suitable advice for growing them in the open fields. He also knew how to store the tubers. At the end of the section about the potato, he warmly acknowledged the works of the most famous of the Protestant botanists, Charles de l'Ecluse (1525-1609), using his Latin name, 'Clusius', and emphasising Clusius' interest in the 'Indian race' of plants from the New World.

Clusius had travelled throughout Europe and was living in Antwerp at the time potatoes were imported from the Canaries. His two main books were printed in Antwerp by the Plantin house. In 1573, he left Antwerp, where the Spanish repression was still raging, and went to Vienna. Here he entered the service of the Emperor Maximilian of Austria, Philip II's uncle and head of the Holy Roman Empire. In Vienna in 1588, when he had left the imperial service, he received potato seeds and tubers from Philip de Sivry, a Flemish prefect. He described them in great detail in his book *Historia (Rariorum plantarum Historia)*, published by Plantin in 1601. He was thus the first botanist to publish anything about the potato on Spanish soil. At no point in this work does Clusius say there might be potatoes in Spain, although he was a frequent visitor to the country and had written a book called *Flora of Spain*. In all

The watercolour Philip de Sivry gave to Clusius with the inscription 'Taratoufli a Phillip de Sivry acceptum Viennae 26 Januarii 1588, Papas Peruänum, Petri Ciecae'

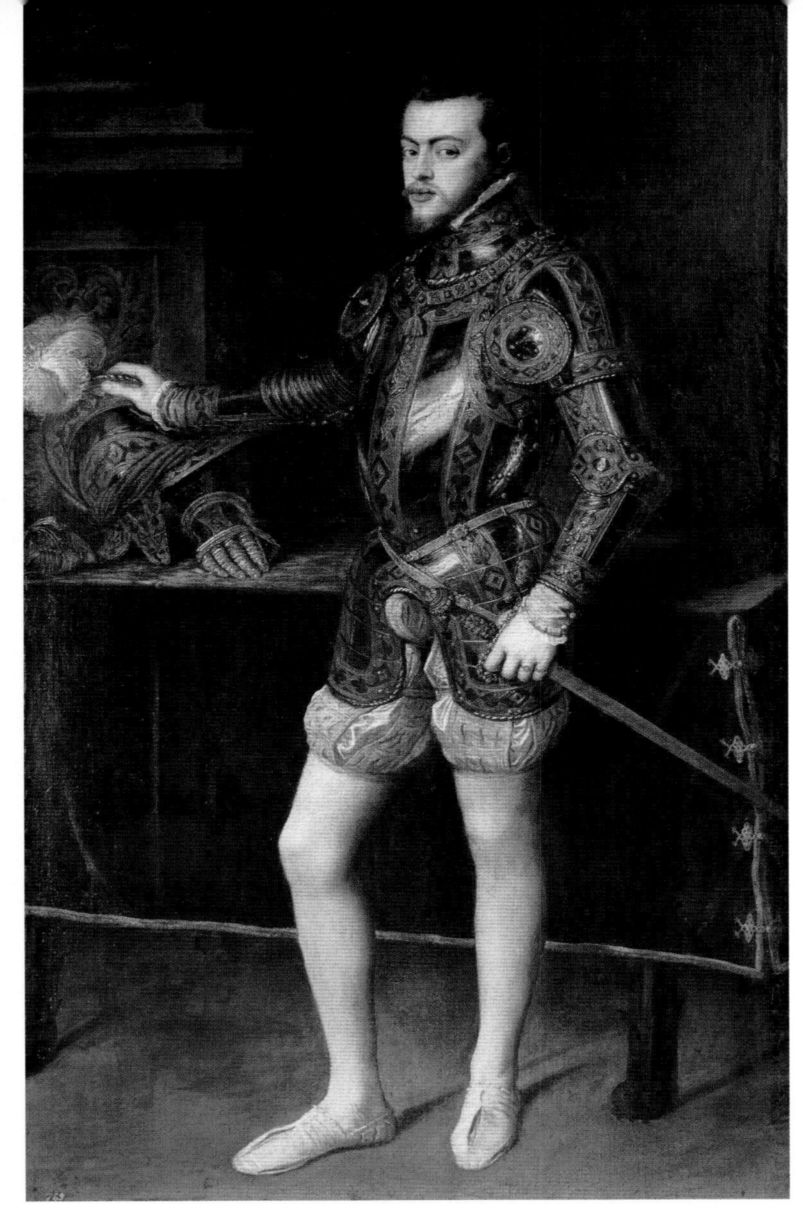

Philip II of Spain (1527-1598), by Titian

probability this silence was a mark of solidarity with his friend Monardes, whose works he translated. He knew that one did not talk about the potato with impunity on Spanish territory. His book was therefore full of contradictions.

He started out by saying that he had not known about the plant before and insisted that he could not understand how the information had escaped his notice, and later, that he recognised that its cultivation was widespread. 'The potato,' he wrote, 'is so common in some areas of Italy that the leftovers are fed to the pigs. Nevertheless, it is all the more remarkable that it is not known in Padua. But today, owing to its high yield, it has reached the gardens of Germany.' His comment about Padua is odd given that the botanical garden in Padua was one of the centres for special studies of rare plants, including those from the New World.

Moreover, he made it clear that he was well aware of the links between the potato and Spain, since he cited printed sources on the tuber that had appeared in Spanish - works written by Spaniards from the New World. Indeed, he mentioned López de Gomara's book, *Historia general de las Indias (General History of the Indies)*, published in 1552, and referred to the works of Pedro Cieza de León (c.1520-1554), known in Latin as *Pietri Ciecae*, one of the first Spanish chroniclers in Peru to have come across the potato. He translated a Latin extract where Cieza de León described the potato and the chuño in the area around Quito, today the capital of Ecuador. Cieza de León had published his book in 1553 in Seville. It had been printed twice in 1555 in Antwerp and appeared in Italian the same year in Rome.

Another sign of his unease with the potato's Hispano-American origins was that he made use of an image (see plate opposite) to associate the potato with the Spanish Empire. In 1589, Clusius had received an excellent botanical watercolour from Philip de Sivry representing a flowering potato stem with fruits and tubers either side. De Sivry had acquired the painting from a friend of the papal legate in Flanders. You can still see the inscription on the watercolour today: 'Taratouffli a Philip de Sivry acceptum Viennae 26 Januarii 1588, Papas Peruänum, Petri Ciecae'. Clusius chose to mention it in his book to reveal Spain's links with the potato without appearing to do so. Pondering the provenance of this image (although he had not wondered where the potato came from), he could not help letting slip another contradiction: 'The Italians no longer remember, but it is certain that this reached them [the papal legate and his entourage] either from Spain or from America.' This was the only time he mentioned the word Spain. He also tells us that the Italians called the plant *taratouffli*.

A Latin baptism

In the same period (1596) there appeared in Basel, where the Reformation had gained acceptance in 1529 and which also used its printing presses to broadcast Humanist ideas, the work of another great Protestant botanist, Gaspard Bauhin (1560-1624), called *Phytopinax*, which gave a detailed description of the potato plant. He mentioned that he had been given its seeds, that the plant was called variously 'Spaniards' *pappas*' and 'Indies *pappas*' and that a doctor from Wroclaw (now Breslau in Poland) had sent him a magnificent colour drawing of the plant, but without fruits or tubers and bearing the inscription *Papas hispanorum*. He sent this drawing to Clusius.

Up to now, the potato had clearly not gained scientific recognition. The same could not be said of other plants from the New World, like tomatoes, tobacco and sunflowers, which already had scientific descriptions and names, and which, what was more, had been studied and named by Spaniards or Italians. Faced with this scientific void and despite their lack of control over the potato, Protestants staked their claim by writing about and publishing on the tuber, and one of them Gaspard

Double flowers of the Duke of York, a very old cultivar

Bauhin saw it as his duty to name it. One can only suppose that this was somehow connected to the political and religious conflicts of the period. Bauhin baptised the potato *Solanum tuberosum* after the similarities he noted with other members of the Solanace family, like the tomato and the aubergine.

In his *Prodromos Theatri Botanici* published in 1620, he claimed that the drawing he had given to Clusius had been sent to him in 1590 and that at the time he had not been able to find a description of the plant. He also observed that plants with double flowers were noted in Austria, and he gave the names used by the Spanish chroniclers of the New World, *papas*, and the Italian name *tartoffoli*.

In his advice about how to grow potatoes, Bauhin set out the methods practised by the Burgundians. They consisted in covering the above-ground stems to encourage the buds to form and increase the number of tubers. This method of cultivation was exactly the same as that prescribed by Olivier de Serres in his work of 1600. The Burgundians belonged to the Franche Comté which, since 1556, had been under Spanish rule and was no longer part of the Duchy of Burgundy. Spanish military convoys crossed the Franche Comté on their way to Flanders (see map, p25). The potatoes produced in this area were used to feed Philip II's troops.

Philip II had a particular interest in the Franche-Comté because it lay at one of the major communication crossroads of the period, and in its capital city, Besançon, lived his bankers and Genoan merchants who controlled the flow of Peruvian silver. In 1535, these men began to organise European high finance meetings. In 1579, the meetings were moved to Piacenza in Italy. Only Europe's richest merchants could attend; they numbered 200 in all, most of them Italians. As Fernand Braudel wrote in *Material Civilization, Economy and Capitalism:* 'They [these rich Italian merchants] were responsible for the early splendour of Seville and Lisbon. They were involved in founding Antwerp and later in the early rise of Frankfurt. They ended up in charge of the Genoese Fairs, known as the Besançon Fairs.' The merchants were the bearers of letters of exchange drawn on the wondrous cargos of the fleet from the Indies.

To sum up: in fifty years, from 1573 to 1620, the potato had spread throughout Europe to Poland and Austria via Spain, France, Italy, England, Switzerland and Germany; the tubers of at least one variety in circulation were ripe at the end of September; the Italians grew so many that they could feed them to pigs; publications on the potato brought out by Protestant scholars like Olivier de Serre, Clusius and Gaspard Bauhin contained all the Italian-sounding vernacular names to refer to it; potatoes were called *cartouffle*, *taratouffli* or *tartoffoli*, and a Protestant scholar had baptised it with a Latin name.

The beginning of the decline of Spanish influence in Europe during the Golden Age was marked by the defeat of the Armada in 1588. Peruvian silver and powerful Spanish armies were not enough to sustain it. The potato, however, was launched and its success would be long lasting.

The potato, a factor of wealth in the modern world

Although the potato was widely grown in vegetable gardens in Europe during the 17th and 18th centuries, in all but a few countries, it was slow to catch on as a crop for the open fields. The major hindrance to its progress was the methods of farming production in force under the Old Regime.

Village communities decided collectively on the alternation of crops and fallow periods. Parcels of land marked out to be sown with wheat were all designated at the same time and for all the landlords. The next year, the same parcels would be sown with a cereal crop that needed less fertile soil (barley, oats, rye or millet in the South) and in the third year, nothing was grown at all. In principle, all the members of the community had the right to graze their livestock on these fallow parcels.

The only fertilizer was animal manure, which was essential to the fertility of the soil. Consequently, all the sown parcels had to become common grazing land after harvesting. But the quantity of manure was insufficient and could not make the soil more fertile.

The major challenge of the time was to introduce new crops that would fulfil this objective. To begin with, in community farming, any change had to receive everyone's consent and benefit everyone. Secondly, although the potato might fulfil this objective, it had the drawback that its leaves were poisonous and could not be used as animal feed once the tubers were consumed. Finally, in a traditional society, suspicion was the rule of the day and lack of information or ignorance meant that anything new was liable to be regarded with distrust. The potato was no exception. It was quickly taken up wholesale, however, after the first attempts at cultivation.

Political and economic factors also played their part. Although people had long been aware of ways of intensifying land use without a fallow period, the peasants had no guarantee that they would find a market for surplus produce and therefore lacked the incentive to apply new methods. There was no efficient national infrastructure that would enable them to send surplus cereals to market, they lacked the financial means to access these markets and they were crushed by taxation systems that shied away from risks and were often limited by lack of currency. The world of politics and taxation needed to be completely overhauled before new crops could be tried.

Public wheat and private potato

The agrarian revolution that accompanied developments in capitalism and agronomic progress removed these problems. Communal fallow periods, common grazing land and crop rotation were swept away by the march of progress with its new roads and waterways, and new urban markets, at which to sell farming surplus, opened up as the peasants moved to the towns. The revolution occurred at different times in different countries: in Europe, the first to be affected were the Low Countries and England; it came later to France; North America set the example, and the entire Eurasian continent as well as South America saw their traditional worlds transformed in the 20th century. Some parts of the Indian subcontinent and Africa are still catching up, but it will not take them long.

Heroes and Myths of the Potato

During the 20th century, the potato was cultivated on a major scale. As farming became increasingly mechanised, it began to be grown in the fields; workers grew it in their gardens, motivated by poverty and the crusade launched by the middle classes to promote the potato among the working class; and in kitchen gardens it was cultivated at every social level. In the 18th century, scientists and the well-to-do had made constant efforts to adopt the potato and did not hesitate to evoke a pantheon of heroes and myths. Popular literature of the 19th century made much of them in almanacs and natural histories. In France, Antoine Augustin Parmentier (1737-1813) who strove to promote the potato is a prime example, and Frederick II of Prussia (1712-1786), enlightened despot, avid reader of history manuals and cultured all-rounder, is another.
Sometimes, authors resorted to fiction. The Spaniard Mellado, who wrote a Diccionairo Universal *(1854), could not help using royalty (Philip II of Spain) and the supreme head of the Church (Pope Pius IV) to promote the potato, recording how the Pope had received potatoes from His Very Catholic Majesty to heal his gout. Mellado skilfully wove his yarn on the frame of the true story of Philip de Sivry's gift of potatoes to Clusius. A long trawl through the Vatican archives by the conservator before the Second World War yielded no evidence for it, but the tale took root and is still wheeled out whenever anyone writes anything about the potato. Also unsubstantiated is the ban placed by the Besançon Parliament on the Burgundians in 1630, forbidding them to eat potatoes which were decreed carriers of leprosy. Parliamentary sessions in Besançon and related edicts for this year show no such ban.*
The potato's champions in England were Sir Francis Drake (1540-1596) and Sir Walter Raleigh (1554-1618), matchless naval commanders, swashbuckling seafarers and no doubt among the great minds of the period, though one too many tricks cost Raleigh his head. The role he played in Virginia in the history of the potato was undoubtedly patriotic but without documented evidence.

Producing surplus crops implied yields greater than demographic growth. What was the connection between agricultural production and demographic growth before the agrarian revolution? Under the Old Regime, yields of cereal crops had been low. However, even before the most immediate effects of the agrarian revolution affected demographic curves, European populations were already clearly on the increase.

With the exception of a few years, the example of France was echoed throughout Europe. In France between 1500 and 1820, for every grain sown, 6.3 grains were harvested. In the same period, the population was steadily growing: in 1515, the country counted about 16 million inhabitants; at the end of the 17th, about 20 million; at the end of the 18th century, 27 million, and in 1820, 30.5 million. The population of France thus continued to grow throughout this period with a steady surge in the last thirty years.

Wheat was widely farmed but was still caught in the vicious cycle of animal fertilizer, fallow land and community pressure. Grain crops demanded a large workforce and big fields, while cabbages and turnips were not sufficiently nourishing. Other, more nutritional supplements could only come from individual crops cultivated out of sight of community greed and the taxman. People could grow what they wanted in their gardens, which were numerous in the towns and protected from prying eyes by walls, and in plots of land allocated to the villagers and also often hidden from the road. Plants from the New World (maize in the South and above all the potato, which was better suited to the European climate) provided plentiful food and took up limited space. With 'home-made' manure, and, for the lucky ones, a cow for its milk, or more likely for the whey (after the butter and cheese had been taken off), and potatoes, the lean periods were over.

So, the potato was probably no stranger to the rise of cottage industry. No need for everyone to go into the fields, and some even rented theirs out and worked at home. Orders for produce came from the town and with them, money, a rarity in a barter economy. The lace-maker on her doorstep, the weaver at his loom are typical images. Fernand Braudel, in the above-named work, points out to his 'attentive traveller', who in June 1775 passed through the villages of the Erzgebirge (a range of mountains between Germany and Czechoslovakia), where girls made lace outdoors: 'The lace-maker's hands are only still to eat a piece of bread or a boiled potato seasoned with a little salt.' Already, the potato had become a fast food: you could eat it without interrupting your work.

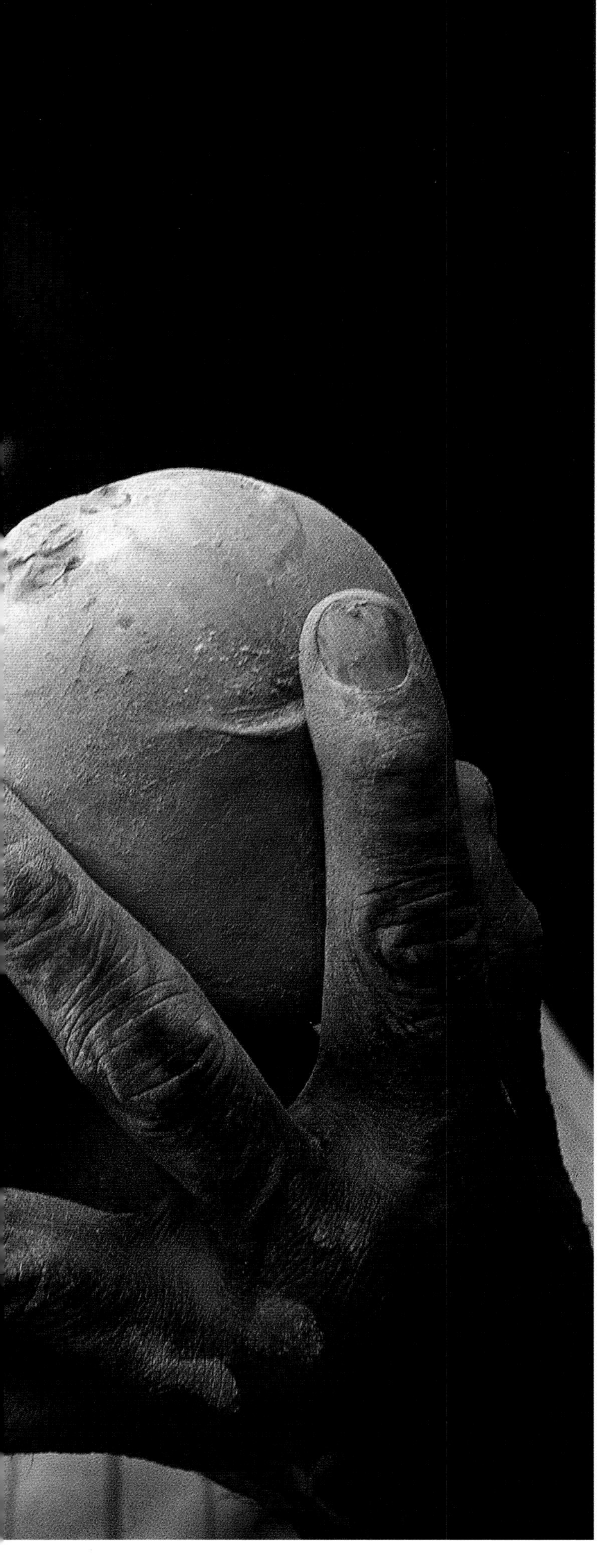

In Asia's green revolution in the 20th century, the potato played a similar role to the one it did in the agrarian revolution in 18th-century Europe (farmer from Himachal Pradesh, India)

This point is confirmed by Arthur Young, the author of a monumental 45-volume portrait of agricultural life in late 18th-century England (*The Annals of Agriculture*). In almost every county, the cottagers, mostly agricultural workers, grew potatoes in their gardens. Market gardening of potatoes for selling in the cities using Irish labour was also very important.

From the middle of the 18th century, the potato gained so much ground in eastern France that it was considered worth levying a tax on it. Potatoes had already largely replaced bread in people's diet without the production of cereals decreasing. By the end of the century, they were being grown throughout the whole of France and the UK. The rise of white bread, the bread of the rich, was becoming more widespread at this period and may also have contributed to the potato's success. Once this expensive habit had taken root, people preferred to add potatoes to their daily diet when times were hard rather than go back to 'black' bread (rye, for example).

In his novel *The Country Doctor*, Honoré de Balzac provided a fictional account of the place the potato occupied in some areas of 19th-century France. The action takes place at the time of the Restoration in the Dauphiné, an area that was quick to adopt the potato as we have seen. At the beginning of the novel, the good doctor and novelist's alter ego describes in detail his energetic day in the village. The population he discovers when he settles in the village lives in total poverty. 'In the middle of this beautiful countryside, the villagers lived in degradation and subsisted on potatoes and dairy products.' This is the potato of self-sufficient survival. Benassis, the doctor, sets out to improve local farming, facilitate transport between the village and nearby Grenoble and sow grain. A potato distillery brings the beginnings of industry to the village, and the potato becomes commercial. The true key to Benassis' success is his agrarian revolution, 'five crop rotations, artificial meadows and the potato.' Potato growing involves new agricultural methods; it is the potato of wealth and the dawn of modernity.

In Europe, the potato progressed most rapidly in Ireland, where Sir Walter Raleigh, Elizabeth I's favouite, owned vast lands. This is why he is often credited with introducing the potato into the country, although there is no official proof that he did. Ireland, with its winds and cool summers (the average daytime temperature is 18°C, lower at night) and its frequent rains, offered the ideal climate for cultivating the potato. The mild autumns encouraged the development of the tubers of the *andigena* potato, with little or no risk of harm from frost. It was thus cultivated very soon after its introduction.

Ireland: a downtrodden colony

At the beginning of the 17th century, after more than a century of wars that had reduced the population by half (first civil war, then war with the English Tudors), Ireland was bled dry. The livestock had been massacred, the woods razed and the fields abandoned. Social chaos reigned and hunger was decimating the survivors. The social and political infrastructure of the country broke down completely. Previously, the Irish had been big consumers of meat and milk, with cereals occupying only a minor place in their diet. Cereals were now exchanged for land and farming rents were paid in grain. For want of other food, the potato fast became important.

The exact date the potato entered the country is not known but it is thought to have arrived from Spain. Spain and Italy, both Catholic countries at war with Protestant England, kept close religious, political and commercial ties with Ireland. Fishing in Irish waters, for instance, was controlled by the Spanish. From the mid-17th century, Cromwell's armies crushed the last Irish resistance, and the victorious English split the best of the country's lands among themselves.

In 1653, the statistics were horrendous: four fifths of the population had died and the rest owed their survival to potatoes. In the second half of the century, the Royal Society publicly praised the merits of the potato which kept the Irish alive. The English Crown sent wheat to landowners, most of whom were English. At the end of the century, the Irish bourgeoisie and aristocracy, who were Catholic, were banned from occupying all professional and spiritual functions. The object was to sever the land's links with its Irish and Catholic past. Legislation affecting the textile and livestock industries finally deprived the Irish of their last vestiges and of any kind of economic future. The new poor flocked to the country, where extortionate rents and a diet consisting exclusively of potatoes awaited them.

Nevertheless, the growth of the Irish population is revealing about the nutritional benefits of potatoes. They sustained the population in wartime (as they did other Europeans in other wars) and when peace returned, they enabled a demographic increase that was unique in Europe. In the mid-18th century, Henry David, an English agricultural expert travelling in the west of Ireland, described in *The Practical Farmer or the Complete English Farmer* (1771), that it was totally natural to see families with ten or more children eating nothing but potatoes. The country recorded a high birth rate and low infant mortality compared to the rest of Europe. The Irish were therefore exceptions. Arthur Young corroborated this information in *A Tour in Ireland* (1780): 'The population is growing excessively and lives on nothing but potatoes and a little milk, with the occasional meat at Christmas and Easter.'

In 1801, the English government, concerned that the revolutions in America and France would resurface in Ireland, passed the Union Act uniting England and Ireland. In reality, the colonial status was set to last. No policy of industrialisation was instituted in Ireland, nor were landowners provided with any incentive to invest and improve their lands or introduce new crops. An ever-growing population continued to settle on cultivable land that was increasingly in demand.

Between 1750 and 1845, the population increased by four million. That year saw the outbreak of *Phytophthora infestans*, a fungus known by its generic name as mildew, which devastated fields of potatoes all over Europe. In the twenty years preceding the ensuing famine, population growth was at one and a half million. The Irish, whose 'daily bread' involved over 3.5kg potatoes per inhabitant per day, would suffer famine, disease and then, from 1846, death or, for the luckier ones, emigration.

Phytophthora infestans: mildew misery

The fungus began its ravages in the course of the summer of 1845; in Poland, Germany, Belgium and France, fields of potatoes had all been affected by September. At the same time, after a cold, rainy summer, the disease struck in Ireland and within days the fields turned black with disease and were rank with the smell of rotting. The tubers were dug up to try to save the crops, but it was too late. Only the very early varieties, grown for export and lifted before the disease struck, were spared. The potatoes eaten by the cottiers, the Lumper variety, not the tastiest but extremely productive and very late, were all lost. The prevalence of the Lumper, a clone (i.e., all the plants were genetically identical) meant that the disease spread quickly.

During the following winter, the English government intervened and sent contributions of wheat. Any remaining potatoes were planted the next year but again, the crops were all destroyed. Weakened by the previous year's famine, the population died in vast numbers from hunger, cholera, typhoid and vitamin deficiencies. Aid provided by the English government, supplemented by convoys of private funds and maize from the United States and Canada, could not keep pace with the enormity and unaccustomed nature of the task and was slowed by profoundly unjust legislation.

The years following the great famine were years of mass emigration, mostly to the United States. Numbers rose as people were driven off the land. The landowning class who until now had exported subsidised wheat to England, went over to raising livestock, suddenly much

A family of cottiers gathered around the pot of potatoes outside their hut (19th-century English engraving)

more profitable, and got rid of unnecessary labourers, casting half a million souls on to the roads. However, the potato still held its own in the Irish diet, and *Phytophythora infestans* continued to strike at regular intervals though no longer with such calamitous results. In Scotland, where social conditions were the same and the dependence on the potato equally prevalent, the consequences were similar.

The ambition of these millions of men and women who lived in the shadow of hunger and disease was to improve their existence and give their children the security of an income that would grant a level of independence in this market economy. Of course, the potato was in no way the answer to all these ills. However nowadays, for many countries with little hope of lasting development, it still represents the first rung on the ladder to prosperity.

If it is to fulfil its potential, the potato needs to be freed from its heavy dependence on chemicals used to combat *Phytophthora infestans*, which has not yet been stamped out. Spores (the reproductive organs of the fungus) appear wherever potatoes are growing and will infect the plants whenever the atmospheric conditions are right. In the 1880s, the French biologist, Alexis Millardet (1838-1902), a vine specialist, produced a non-chemical treatment for mildew called Bordeaux Mixture involving lime and copper sulphate. It was the first preventive treatment for the fungus and was applied to potato fields.

Until the 1990s, *Phytophthora infestans* appeared to be on the wane all over the world. The known form, called A1, a cloned form, was reduced by drastic hygiene measures. Planting disease-free seed potatoes, purging the fields by crop rotation, eliminating tubers still in the ground, removing the leaves before lifting and always using fungicides were the measures brought into force. Depending on the weather conditions and the resistance of the planted cultivar, treatments had to be applied between two and 12 times during the growing period. The CIP, the Potato Centre in Lima (see inset, p36), estimated that chemical treatments cost the world 2 billion dollars a year, of which 600 million went to developing countries with, in addition, the inevitable cost to public health and the environment. The appearance of a new form called A2 broke out a decade ago. This form is resistant to the fungicides being used and is extremely virulent. A1 and

China is now the world's number one potato producer (farmer's son in the province of Sichuan, China)

A2 are now joining forces and reproducing, thereby increasing their genetic stock and making the task of controlling them extremely complex. The new challenge for the potato is to overcome the old predator *Phytophthora infestans*, which acts like the Hydra with its seven heads that grew back as soon as they were cut off. The potato's future depends on this challenge being met.

The potato today

Very few potatoes cross borders: the risk of fungus is too great. Potatoes are therefore consumed in the country in which they are grown and thus give the people a measure of dietary self-sufficiency. Potatoes are now grown in 168 countries, most of them in Africa. Developing countries, particularly in Asia, represent the new growth area. China is the world's number one producer, with over 50 million tonnes a year, and since the 1960s, Asia has gone from producing 10% of the world's share to more than a third.
In tropical regions where potatoes mature very early, only 50 days, compared to an average 150 in temperate zones, are needed to produce comparable yields, and the potato has an established place in the agricultural cycle. The green revolution has reduced the growing time of rice and led to quicker crop rotation. At low altitudes, potato crops are alternated with two rice crops. Indian farmers plant in the autumn but keep their harvests in refrigerators during the hot season. Elsewhere, in southern Asia, urbanisation and rising living standards have led to a decrease in the popularity of rice in favour of the potato. Outside China though, the potato plays an insignificant role in the Asian diet and is mainly fed to animals.

However, the global growth of harvests is slowing. The ground it has gained in the East does not make up for the losses with European consumers. Harvests tripled in Asia in the last forty years but have dropped by nearly 50% in Europe. Even Poland, which holds the world record for consumption per capita, is going off potatoes. Although still the world's number one potato-eater, it has reduced its yearly consumption by half, going from 220 to 125kg for the period 1960 to 2000. Changes in dietary habits are at the root of this disaffection. With improved living standards, Europeans are eating more fruit, vegetables and cereals, and their livestock are fed fewer potatoes than in previous times.

North America is in some ways the potato's 'saviour' in the western world. The number of potatoes consumed per US citizen went up from 49 to 65kg, still for the same period. Harvests have gone from 12.5 million tonnes in the early 1960s to 21.4 million tonnes between 1997 and 1999, showing an increase of nearly 70%. North American animals are fed a negligible amount. In adapting to fast food, an expanding market, the potato has brought off a veritable tour de force. Two thirds of national production is turned into frozen chips, crisps, flakes and other pre-packaged foods, all of which are routinely eaten in North America.

With 1.8 billion tonnes harvested between 1997 and 1999, all the cereal crops put together (rice, wheat and maize) produced half the calories consumed by the world's 5.9 billion people. The potato is a long way behind, with nearly 300 million tonnes picked each year for the same period. But these statistics need qualifying. If you compare yields per hectare and the relation between quantities consumed and nutritional values, the balance is clearly weighted in favour of the potato. For rice, the cereal we eat most of, one hectare gives an average of 3.8 tonnes; the average for potatoes is 16 tonnes per hectare. Still, yields per hectare vary enormously throughout the world. In Central Asia, yields are not above 5 tonnes per hectare; in Western Europe and the United States, they are around 40 tonnes, while Western Australia, where a combination of suitable soils, the absence of predators and irrigation provide optimal conditions, breaks all records with 100 tonnes per hectare.

These figures again need qualifying. A freshly lifted potato contains high water content, whereas rice contains far less. The nutritional value is expressed in dry matter: one hectare of potatoes represents 3.7 tonnes of dry matter, while the same area of rice gives 3.2 tonnes. These statistics are based on world averages. As soon as yields rise, the gap widens. In the United States, where the average yield of one hectare of rice expressed in dry matter is 5.5 tonnes, the potato gives 9 tonnes of dry matter per planted hectare. The same is true for wheat and maize: when they are compared with the potato, the potato always appears to have the advantage.

The nutritional value of the potato

It contains high levels of vitamin C, or ascorbic acid, lack of which causes scurvy. In the past, scurvy ravaged ships' crews during long periods with no fresh fruit or vegetables. Once the potato was introduced into Europe, raw potatoes were eaten during voyages (a few hundred grams are enough to stave off disease). Scurvy, which was prevalent among many peasant communities, has thus disappeared.

The table below (from J. Lang, 'Notes of a Potato Watcher') shows the percentage of daily requirements satisfied in trace elements, vitamins, proteins and calories, for 500g potatoes.

Nutritional elements	Peeled then cooked in water (%)	Unpeeled, cooked in water and eaten with the skin (%)
Calcium	5.6	9.4
Iron	27	41.6
Phosphorus	17.5	25
Potassium	Over 100	Over 100
Vitamin C	Over 100	Over 100
Vitamin A	1.5	1.5
Vitamin B1	30	40
Vitamin B2	2.5	5
Protein		
• Nitrogen	15.5	16.5
• Nicotine acid	15	15
Fat	Trace	Trace
Calories	11.5	11.5

'Charlotte Potatoes in a Salt Crust' by Alain Passard (recipe, page 104)

Complex B vitamins are well represented in the potato, and regular consumption can help prevent nervous and skin disorders, like beri-beri, a B1 deficiency triggered by eating nothing but hulled rice, and pellagra, which largely affects populations that subsist on maize. The excellent carbohydrate content (or slow sugars) in potatoes makes them a high-energy food that is easy to digest. They also contain high levels of protein: a kilo of potatoes provides half the daily adult requirement.

The potato is therefore a complete food. When steamed and eaten with its skin, it retains important nutritional elements; cooked potato skin aids the digestion of other ingested foods, so peeling wastes a quarter of the potato, in terms of both quality and quantity (and flavour!) - there is no doubt that peeling potatoes is a laborious process that harms its nutritional value.

A major asset for the potato, compared with cereals, is the ease of preparing it. Rice and wheat need to be dried after harvesting, then the ears have to be shelled and the grains hulled while wheat must be ground or crushed; only maize can be eaten without these labour-intensive stages. Then they need to have water added and a receptacle to cook them before they can be eaten. The potato can do without all this. It requires no more than a fire once it has been dug up. Very little space has to be set aside to grow enough potatoes to feed a family of six for a year: one foot is enough for one or two kilos of tubers. They can be harvested over time, and the early crops can even stay in the ground provided the soil is free from predators. Very little time is needed to cultivate them and the yields are proportionally very high.

The politically correct potato

Malnutrition is the result of insufficient food or of the body not making effective use of the food during metabolism, or of a combination of the two. Undernourished people are rarely suffering simply from lack of protein. It is the low level of energy matter in their diet, principally carbohydrates, that first needs to be tackled. Plants with tubers, especially potatoes, can provide this precious supplement and are high in both carbohydrates and proteins for moderate outlay.

In the fight against famine, scientific developments can use *andigena* potatoes to select new types. In recent years, the CIP has carried out research to find potatoes that are likely to answer to farmers' needs in developing countries. Wild species, like the traditional potato varieties, can provide genes that will enable potatoes to be cultivated in increasingly varied climates and soils, without involving an unacceptable cost in terms of fungicides and pesticides to both the environment and the farmers. Some quite simple improvements could aid the evolution of potato growing, such as virus-free seeds, a better approach to soil or greater understanding of crop cycles. Trial cultivars are planted each year and research for new ones is an ongoing task.

A centre with an international vocation

The International Potato Centre (CIP) was founded in Lima in 1971 where it has its headquarters. A non-profit-making institute for scientific research, it has as its mission to increase the agricultural potential of the potato, the sweet potato and other roots and tubers in developing countries. The CIP's main objectives are to reduce poverty, ensure food safety and improve the management of natural resources in the Andes and other mountainous regions.
Interdisciplinary teams are working in more than 30 countries to develop the most locally suitable solutions to the manifold problems associated with growing and eating roots and tubers, as well as to the management of natural resources.
The world potato gene bank, financed by the CIP, which has 5,000 types of wild and cultivated potato, as well as a vast collection of sweet potatoes and Andean roots and tubers, can help save species that are at risk of dying out.
In the Andes, the cradle of the potato and roots and tubers that represent a unique heritage, the CIP is working with village communities to preserve the biodiversity. Andean farmers grow more than 4,000 species of indigenous potato of an astonishing variety of shape, colour and flavour whose vitamin content and culinary potential represent excellent possibilities for sources of revenue. The CIP undertakes research projects in conjunction with farmers, on the one hand to make research answer to the requirements of the market and on the other to help them produce indigenous potatoes that will preserve biodiversity and find commercial outlets.

The Potato Garden

The Potato Garden

A field of flowering potatoes in Scotland

Preceding pages: Ratte flowers

Among the responses to the great famine in Ireland were the programmes initiated after 1850 to reintroduce genes from wild species, in other words, those of essentially Andean origin. The aim was to improve the resistance of European cultivars with a weak genetic heritage that had become susceptible to mildew (*Phytophtora infestans*). Potato gardeners, like all gardeners, must make way for the complexity of wild plants, which are a crucial source of strength. Gardens need both the expertise and experience harboured in domesticated plants and the element of surprise and vitality afforded by wild species.

Resistant cultivars

The principles of potato cultivation are based on choosing resistant cultivars (plants selected for specific features). Healthy seed potatoes, crop rotation and quality care of the soil should be the potato gardener's first concerns. The seed tubers should be certified disease-free. Potatoes, like many cultivated plants are prone to a number of pathologies. Some, like viruses, or virus-induced illnesses, often transmitted by greenfly, are impossible to treat. Numbers of clones can be created by taking a few cells from the meristem (the tissue at the tip of the bud) from a healthy plant and growing it in a sterile environment. For other varieties where potatoes are affected by viruses, heat treatments now exist that stop the virus developing without arresting plant growth.

If you buy healthy tubers, go for pre-germinated ones. If the weather stops you planting immediately, keep the tubers out of the frost and light but don't wait too long before putting them in the ground. You should also choose varieties for their resistance to diseases like mildew, which is a very real danger today and needs to be fought with determination. Bear in mind that in the garden, as in everything, diversity is the best protection against adversity. Predators (viruses, bacteria, fungus and insects) are more likely to attack preys whose genetic heritage is familiar to them. This is the disadvantage of cloned plants. Once the defence system is undermined in a cloned plant, all the other plants of the same clone are at risk. So by planting several cultivars and mixing your potatoes, as Andean farmers do, you will be helping to

Potato flowers

Email order for potato seedlings ready to be planted out (see Address Book, page 191)

keep predators at bay. In addition, you will also be providing yourself with a range of potatoes for different recipes and will be able to store them for longer periods. A resistant cultivar increases its chances of a healthy, tubiferous life if it is planted in healthy soil. Don't forget that humans can move about but plants don't have legs. All their resources need to be drawn from one spot. They are quite capable of doing this provided you give them the opportunity. They will look after finding the necessary energy for their development, but it is up to you to do the rest and give them a well-structured soil and a life-enhancing environment.

A sprouting potato

A balanced ecology

A well-structured soil includes minerals required for plant growth, completely decomposed organic matter, active flora and fauna and water. The minerals come from the decomposed organic matter. For your plants to reap the benefits, you need an army of soil workers. Earthworms on the frontline, associated with those other essential organisms, battalions of bacteria, regiments of fungus and a corps of insects all produce minerals in their best form for plant metabolism. This is called worm compost at the garden nursery. It is like black gold: friable and odourless but expensive (rightly so), so use it sparingly. If you put down organic matter (only ever on the surface) the worms and all the other workers will do the rest free of charge. But you must give them a constant supply of whatever vegetable matter you can lay your hands on, broken down as fine as possible: fallen leaves, grass cuttings, green waste from your kitchen, hedge cuttings from next door and straw. This is called mulching, from the old English, 'melsc' meaning soft.

Spread the mulch around the plants in mixed layers to help decomposition and you can be sure of a cycle of organic molecules ready to decompose and dependent on underground life. Worms make their way to the surface and attack the mulch, creating numerous tiny tunnels as they go that help the water circulate and airs the ground; plants need air around their roots. The decomposed organic matter acts like a sponge by retaining water, and the mulch stops the water evaporating. You won't have to water the plants, and in any case, watering them with treated water (i.e., drinking water) will leave traces of chlorine,

When planting, you can measure the distance between plants with your feet

Flowers from the cultivar Maris Piper

which is harmful to all the life going on in the compost. Drinking water is precious; men drink it, not plants. You should never see the surface of the earth, which should always be covered in mulch at least 5cm thick although 10cm is better.

Mulch provides an ideal home for predators, but it is also inhabited by predators' predators. A silent and relentless battle goes on, a barely visible orgy where the bigger ones eat the smaller and the smallest parasites eat the big ones until they are all dead and everything decomposes. This is called balanced ecology and is a self-supporting system. Spiders, tiny wasps, beetles and their voracious larvae, fungus that preys on insects and fungus that preys on other fungus represent a whole crucial life. A few toads and hedgehogs are always welcome and will sort out your slugs and snails. Don't use slug pellets: hedgehogs, birds and other small mammals will die as a result and you will be killing off other garden helpers needlessly. And make way for moles. In short, you should let everything live. A plant under attack is an unbalanced plant, which means that you have made a wrong decision either about your plant or about its site. No digging: you can exercise your muscles and relations with your neighbours by fetching constant supplies of vegetable waste.

How to plant

Provided the plants are healthy and the soil well-structured, well-drained and kept cool and moist under the mulch, all you have to do is plant. Avoid heavy soils: potatoes like sandy, well-drained soil. Good use of mulch year after year is an excellent way of making the soil less heavy. The best moment is the spring, but wait for the soil to warm up, when the grass begins to grow. Potatoes are sensitive to frost and you should keep an eye on the weather forecast and protect young plants from the slightest chill. In the warmest climates you can plant up to four weeks ahead; further north and east you should wait as long as possible. The best place is one that gets as much light as possible. Potatoes like open space with no shadow from trees or high walls. If you are planting potatoes in a plot for the first time, get rid of the weeds and till the surface, burying any clods and little plants still in them. Then spread your mulch.

Once you have entirely covered the plot with mulch and are ready to plant, leave plenty of space around each potato: a square metre or 100cm between each plant and between rows if you are planting a lot of plants. You will find this space useful to work in for mulching and banking up, and if the plants are not touching, there is less chance

Freshly lifted new potato with delicate skin

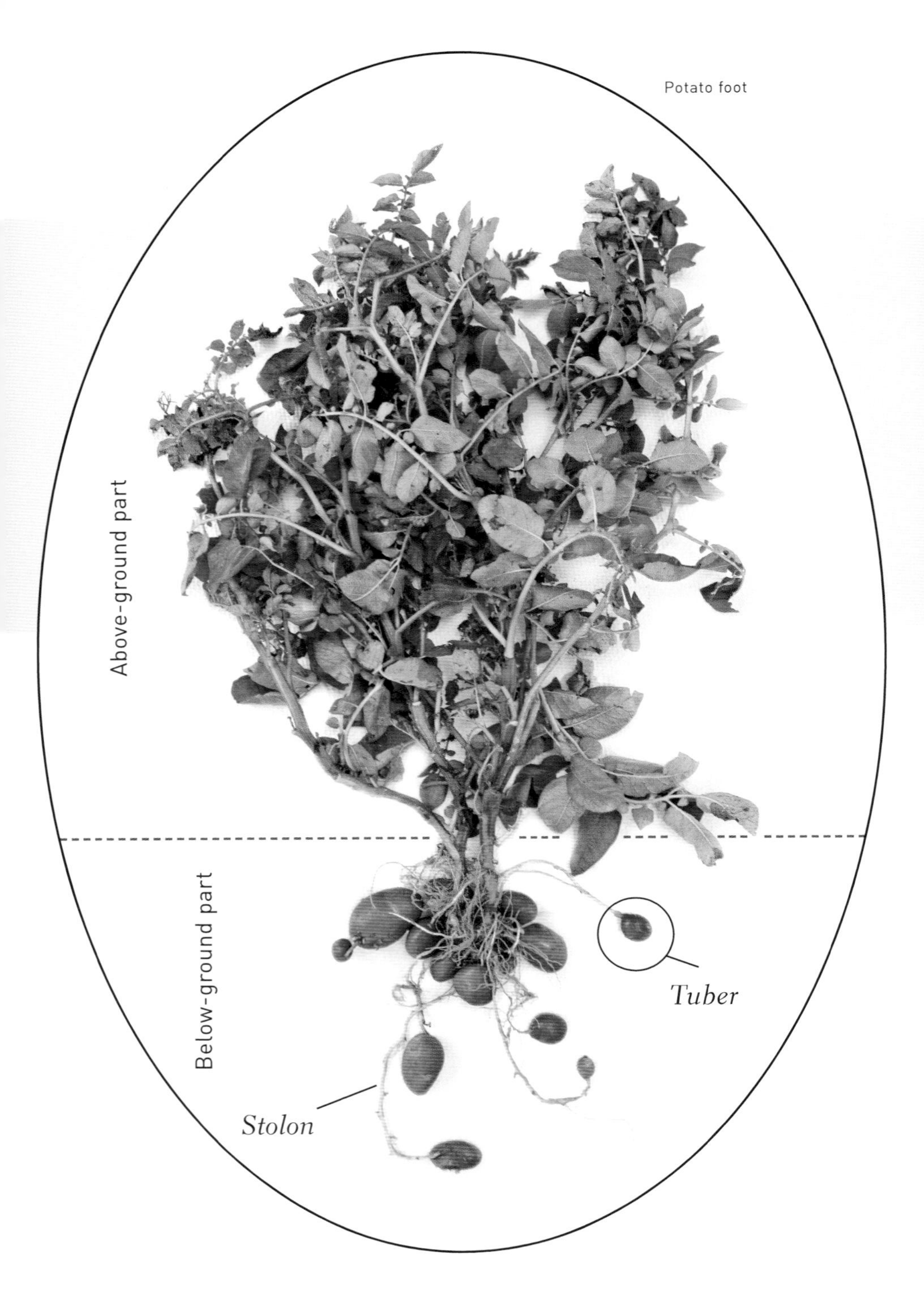

Don't forget to label your potato garden

before harvesting (the time you harvest will depend on your choice of plant).

What to plant

New potatoes can be lifted as soon as they are mature, but only collect what you need as they will go on growing for a while without losing any of their qualities. The late varieties are generally lifted in September when the tuber is mature. For best keeping, lift late potatoes when they are fully mature. Lift in dry, windy weather for the potatoes to dry quickly, without exposing them too long to the light. They will quickly turn green in the light and become unusable. Store in a cool, dry place protected from frost and cover them in straw or sacking. Make sure they are somewhere where the air can circulate. Potatoes are among the easiest plants to grow.

of disease spreading and they will be happier. Lift some mulch to uncover the surface; dig lightly with a trowel; put your tuber with the shoots (the buds) sticking up, then cover them over and put back the mulch.

Potato roots grow very close to the surface, and you need to bank up to encourage the roots and tubers to develop. When the plants are 30cm high, bank up by placing earth around the stem over the mulch to halfway up. Then remulch. You can bank up again a fortnight later. This way, the harvest will be more plentiful and the potatoes easy to lift, because they will stay on the surface. If the summer is rainy with cool days, you need to treat them for mildew with a solution of Bordeaux Mixture. Do this twice every two weeks. Cut the leaves off the plants a week

Colorado potato beetle (*Leptinotarsa decemlineata*). Treat with nettle manure

The big tuber in the middle is the seed tuber from which the plant grew

Harvesting your potatoes

New potatoes: *these are the first potatoes of the season. They mature quickly, after about ten weeks, have a delicate skin and are not good keepers so they should be eaten straight after lifting. Plant them from mid-March to the end of May and harvest in May to the end of July.*
Mid-season potatoes: ready from the middle to the end of July. Bigger than new potatoes and are generally good keepers.
Autumn potatoes: *cultivated to keep during the winter, with high yields. They are big with a thick skin. Mid-season potatoes should be planted from mid-March to the end of April and lifted from mid-July to the end of September/early October. If you have trouble with slugs, lift all the autumn potatoes as soon as possible, before the autumn rains.*

They are ideal for beginners and can even be grown in pots, but you should choose new varieties with small tubers and use a big pot, about 30cm in diameter.

A few words about phytophysiology

Potatoes form on a below-ground stem called a rhizome. The resulting growth is the tuber which constitutes a source of nutrients. The stems that develop at the surface are called the stolons and can also bear potatoes. This is what happens when plants are raised from seed. The potato is studded with tiny axillary buds or 'eyes' surrounded by invisible leaves. It is these that produce the shoots. This capacity for budding means that a single potato can produce a lot of plants. For this, you should cut the tuber into pieces with an eye in each one (to be avoided for phytosanitary reasons).
The flowers are star-shaped with a symmetric corolla made up of five petals that are fused at the base. The stamens are red, yellow or orange and very obvious. They end with anthers, also fused, in a cone around the stigma (the tip of the pistil). The tips of the petals curve outwards. Fertilisation is autogamous.
The colour varies according to the variety, from bright white through shades of lavender and lilac to dark blue. They are perfumed and bear a striking resemblance to other flowers in the Solanace family, like the tomato, aubergine or tobacco. The fruit of the potato is like a small green tomato.

Potato Portraits

All Blue

For hungry gardeners

Some rare varieties, either very old or recently introduced, do not have their complete descriptions. However, we consider them important for biodiversity.

Accent

Very early (lift in April)
Origin: Holland, 1994
Availability: England and Holland
Uses: boil or fry
Features: oval or round, medium sized, with smooth, bright yellow skin, firm flesh and smell of rotting.
(Photo p.51)

Accord

Very early
Origin: Holland, 1996
Features: oval with white cracked flesh, shallow eyes and a distinctive flavour.
(Photo p.52)

Admiral
Very early
Origin: United Kingdom, 1998
Uses: all types of cooking
Features: wide with smooth white skin, cream, very firm flesh and shallow eyes.

Agria
Mid-season to early
Origin: West Germany, 1995
Availability: Canada, New Zealand, Switzerland and United Kingdom
Uses: boil, bake, chips, fry, purée, sauté or roast
Features: oval, good size, dark yellow in colour with an excellent flavour.

Ailsa
Mid-season to early
Origin: Scotland, 1984
Availability: United Kingdom
Uses: boil, fry, purée or for chips
Features: round or oval, medium sized with light skin, pearly white flesh and a floury texture. Good flavour.

Ajax
Early
Origin: Holland
Availability: Holland, Pakistan and Vietnam
Uses: boil, roast and fry
Features: oval with smooth, yellow skin and firm pale yellow flesh. Not much flavour.

Alcmaria
Very early (lift in April)
Origin: Holland, 1970
Availability: all types of cooking
Features: long and oval with yellow skin and firm flesh. Shallow eyes.

Alex
Early
Origin: Denmark, 1995
Availability: Europe and United Kingdom
Uses: for salads and all types of cooking
Features: white skin with blue patches. Pearly white firm flesh with shallow eyes.

All Blue
Mid-season
Origin: United States
Availability: United States and United Kingdom
Uses: bake, roast and fry
Features: long and oval with dark purplish-blue skin and blue flesh.

Anna
Mid-season, early
Origin: Ireland, 1996
Availability: Ireland and United Kingdom
Uses: boil and bake
Features: uniform with very light skin and pearly white floury flesh. Mostly sold pre-packed.

Ambo | Admiral | Claret (p. 53)

Ambo
Mid-season to early
Origin: Ireland, 1993
Availability: Ireland, New Zealand, Switzerland and United Kingdom
Uses: boil and bake
Features: pearly white skin, very light flesh and big pink eyes. Floury without much flavour.

Aminca
Very early (lift in April)
Origin: Holland, 1977
Availability: Denmark, Italy and United Kingdom
Uses: boil, bake or for chips
Features: oval, medium wide with bright yellow skin and flesh. Deep eyes and high dry- matter content. Widely used for making chips.

Anya
Early
Origin: Scotland, 1997
Availability: United Kingdom
Uses: boil, for salads
Features: shaped like a long oval finger, small and irregular with rose-beige skin and firm white flesh. Tastes of fresh nuts.

Appell
Mid-season
Origin: Sweden, 1997
Availability: Sweden and United Kingdom
Uses: for chips, flakes and starch extraction
Features: oval with yellow skin.
(Photo p.50)

Argos
Very early
Origin: Scotland, 1994
Availability: United Kingdom
Features: round to oval with white skin, firm cream flesh and deep eyes. Very delicate, crumbles easily.
(Photo p.50)

Arran Banner
Early, very early
Origin: Scotland, 1927
Availability: Cyprus, New Zealand, Portugal and United Kingdom
Uses: boil
Features: round to oval with white skin, firm pearly white flesh and deep eyes.

Arran Comet
Very early (lift in April)
Origin: Scotland, 1957
Availability: United Kingdom
Uses: boil and for chips
Features: round to oval with white skin, cream flesh and deep eyes. Very good new potato, difficult to find.

Arran Consul
Early, very early
Origin: Scotland, 1925
Availability: United Kingdom
Uses: boil, bake, purée and roast
Features: round with very bright skin, cream flesh and very deep eyes. Recognised as 'the potato that helped win the war'.

Arran Pilot
Very early
Origin: Scotland, 1930
Availability: United Kingdom
Uses: average for all types of cooking
Features: oval, bean-shaped with white skin and flesh, and shallow eyes. Its texture is a bit floury. Discolours when cooked and crumbles easily. After its introduction in 1931 in Great Britain, it was the most popular of the very early potatoes for thirty years.

Arran Victory or Irish Blues
Mid-season
Origin: Scotland, 1918
Availability: United Kingdom
Uses: bake, boil, roast and other types of cooking
Features: oval with dark purple skin, bright white floury flesh, and deep eyes. The oldest variety and the most highly flavoured of the Arrans still available.

Ausonia
Early
Origin: Holland, 1981
Availability: Greece, Holland and United Kingdom
Uses: boil, bake and for all types of cooking
Features: oval with white skin and bright yellow, floury flesh.

Avalanche
Very early
Origin: Northern Ireland, 1989
Availability: United Kingdom (rarely found)
Uses: boil and purée
Features: round or oval, medium sized with pearly white flesh, firm texture and sweetish flavour.
(Photo p.53)

Bintje

Argos (p. 49)

Appell (p. 49) | Arran Victory | Cosmos (p. 53)

Atlantic
Mid-season, early
Origin: United States, 1978
Availability: Australia, Canada, United States (North Carolina), New Zealand
Uses: boil, bake, fry, purée, roast or for chips
Features: round to oval with rough, light chamois-coloured skin and white flesh. Widely used for making chips.

Avondale
Mid-season to early
Origin: Ireland, 1982
Availability: Canaries, Egypt, Hungary, Israel, Morocco, Pakistan, Portugal, Spain, Sri Lanka and United Kingdom
Uses: all types of cooking
Features: round or oval with pale beige skin. Its pearly white flesh is soft and firm.

Accent (p. 48) | Arran Comet | Belle de Fontenay | Arran Pilot

Balmoral
Early
Origin: Ireland, 1991
Availability: Ireland and United Kingdom
Uses: boil, bake, purée and roast
Features: oval with red and white skin and dark cream flesh. Softish flesh with shallow eyes. When boiled it discolours slightly and crumbles easily.
(Photo p.53)

Barna
Mid-season to late
Origin: Ireland, 1993
Availability: Ireland and United Kingdom
Uses: boil or roast
Features: oval and regular with red skin and white, firmish, warm-feeling flesh that tastes of fresh nuts.

Belle de Fontenay, Boulangère Henaut
Very early
Origin: France, 1885
Availability: Australia, France and United Kingdom
Uses: boil, purée or for salads
Features: long with pale yellow skin and firm yellow flesh. Tastes of fresh butter. A classic in French cooking and improves with keeping. Don't hesitate to eat the skin.

BelRus
Mid-season to late
Origin: United States, 1978
Availability: Canada, United States (north-east States and north Florida)
Uses: bake, for chips, purée or roast
Features: long all over with thick dark skin and pearly white flesh. Excellent for cooking, especially steamed or in gratins. When roast, its skin goes deliciously crispy.

BF 15
Early
Origin: France, 1947
Availability: France
Uses: boil or for salads
Features: long with firm yellow skin and flesh. Excellent flavour. Derived from Belle de Fontenay.

Bintje
Very early
Origin: Holland, 1910
Availability: Australia, Brazil, Canada, Denmark, Finland, Italy, Holland, New Zealand, Sweden, Thailand and United Kingdom
Uses: boil, bake, for chips, purée, roast or in salads
Features: long and oval with pale yellow skin and flesh. Has a very distinctive flavour. Widely used for making chips.

Accord (p. 48) | Concord | BF15

Bishop
Mid-season to late
Origin: United Kingdom, 1912
Availability: United Kingdom
Uses: boil, roast or for salads
Features: shaped like a large bean with white skin and flesh. Tastes like fresh nuts.

British Queen(s)
Early
Origin: Scotland, 1894
Uses: boil, bake, purée or roast
Features: shaped like a large bean with white skin and flesh. Its texture is a bit dry and floury but it has an excellent flavour. Keeps its flavour if cooked with the skin.

CalWhite
Mid-season to early
Origin: United States, 1997
Availability: Canada, United States (California and Idaho)
Uses: bake, purée or for chips
Features: oblong with white skin and flesh.

Cara White and Red
Mid-season to late
Origin: Ireland, 1976
Availability: Cyprus, Egypt, Ireland, Israel and United Kingdom
Uses: boil, bake, for chips and all types of cooking
Features: round or oval with white skin and pink eyes. Its pale yellow flesh is soft and firm. There is a variety with pink skin and pearly white flesh.
(Photo p.54)

Carlingford
Very early (harvest in April)
Origin: Northern Ireland, 1982
Availability: Australia and United Kingdom
Uses: boil, bake and for chips
Features: round or oval with white skin and flesh. Medium-sized shallow eyes. Its texture is firm with a distinctive flavour. An excellent new potato and very good steamed or microwaved.

Catriona and Blue Catriona
Early
Origin: Scotland, 1920. Blue Catriona: United Kingdom 1979
Availability: United Kingdom
Uses: boil, bake and for all types of cooking
Features: shaped like a large bean with white skin and pretty mauve patches around big eyes. Pale yellow flesh with excellent, strongish flavour.

Celine
Early to very early
Origin: Scotland, 1999
Uses: bake and for all types of cooking
Features: oval with red skin and bright yellow flesh, slightly floury with shallow oval eyes.
(Photo p.54)

Centennial Russet
Mid-season to early
Origin: United States, 1977
Availability: United States (California, Colorado, Idaho, Oregon, Texas, Washington)
Uses: boil, bake and purée
Features: oval to oblong with thick dark speckled skin, white floury flesh and shallow eyes.

Champion
Mid-season to late
Origin: United Kingdom, 1876
Availability: No longer on the market but can be found in collections
Uses: excellent for all types of cooking
Features: round with white skin and yellow flesh. Excellent flavour.

Charlotte, Noirmoutier
Mid-season to early
Origin: France, 1981
Availability: boil, bake or in salads
Features: pear-shaped, long and oval with firm, pale yellow skin and a flavour reminiscent of chestnut. Excellent when boiled.

Cherie
Early to very early
Origin: United Kingdom, 1997
Availability: United Kingdom
Features: long and oval with red skin, bright yellow flesh and shallow eyes.

Chieftain
Mid-season
Origin: United States, 1996
Availability: Canada, United States
Uses: boil and bake
Features: round or oblong with smoothish, bright red skin and white flesh.

Chipeta
Mid-season to late
Origin: United States, 1993
Availability: Canada, United States (Colorado and Idaho)
Uses: boil, bake, purée or for chips
Features: round with white skin with reddish patches and pearly white flesh. Often used for making chips.

Cleopatra
Very early (lift in April)
Origin: Holland, 1980
Availability: Algeria, Hungary
Uses: boil
Features: oval with pink skin and red mottling and dense pale yellow flesh.

Colleen
Very early
Origin: Ireland, 1993
Features: oval with white skin, firm flesh and shallow eyes.

Colmo
Very early (lift in April)
Origin: Holland
Availability: Holland and United Kingdom
Uses: Boil but good for all types of cooking
Features: roundish or oval with white skin and firm yellow flesh.

Concord
Very early
Origin: Holland, 1988
Availability: Holland and United Kingdom
Uses: suitable for all types of cooking
Features: long with yellow skin and flesh and deep eyes. Fragile and discolours with cooking.

Congo
Mid-season to late
Origin: Congo
Availability: Australia, United Kingdom (only available to determined gardeners)
Uses: boil, purée or in salads
Features: small, delicate and knobbly with shiny deep purplish-black skin and beetroot-black flesh. Not much flavour.

Cosmos
Early
Origin: Holland, 1997
Features: oval with yellow skin and soft dark cream flesh with deep eyes.
(Photo p.50)

Colleen

Claret
Very early
Origin: Scotland, 1996
Availability: Scotland
Uses: suitable for all types of cooking
Features: round to oval with smooth, pinkish-red skin and firm pearly white flesh.

Cherie

Carlingford Balmoral (p. 51) Claret
Avalanche (p. 50) Catriona

Celine (p. 52) Désirée
Cara White (p. 52) Arran Banner (p. 50)

Delcora
Very early
Origin: Holland, 1988
Availability: boil, for chips or salads
Features: long and oval with pink and red skin and bright yellow flesh. Very tasty and also not floury.

Désirée
Mid-season to early
Origin: Holland, 1962
Availability: Algeria, America, Argentina, Australia, Cameroon, Chile, Holland, Iran, Ireland, Malawi, Morocco, New Zealand, Portugal, Sri Lanka, Pakistan, Tunisia and United Kingdom
Uses: suitable for all types of cooking
Features: oval with light red skin, firm pale yellow flesh and shallow eyes. Very tasty. Without contest the most popular red potato in the world.

Diamant
Very early
Origin: Holland, 1982
Availability: Cameroon, Canada, Egypt, New Zealand and Pakistan
Uses: boil and bake
Features: long and oval with rough skin, firm yellow flesh and a nutty flavour.

Ditta
Early
Origin: Australia, 1950
Availability: Australia, Holland and United Kingdom
Uses: boil and roast
Features: long and oval with rough brown skin and firm pale yellow flesh. When cooked it tastes of butter and melts in the mouth.

Dr McIntosh
Very early
Origin: United Kingdom, 1944
Availability: New Zealand and United Kingdom (quite rare now)
Uses: boil, bake, quite good for other types of cooking
Features: long and oval with bright white skin and creamy flesh.

Draga
Early
Origin: Holland, 1970
Availability: Iran, New Zealand
Uses: boil, purée or in salads but also good for all other types of cooking
Features: round with white and yellow skin. Firm texture, very tasty and melts in the mouth.

Duke of York, Eersteling
Very early (lift in April)
Origin: Scotland, 1891
Availability: France, Holland and United Kingdom
Uses: boil and good for other types of cooking
Features: long, oval and pear-shaped with pale yellow skin and firm, bright yellow flesh. Excellent sweet flavour, quite strong. Should be eaten young.

Duke of York Red, Rode Eersteling
Very early (lift in April)
Origin: Holland, 1842
Availability: Holland and United Kingdom (quite rare)
Uses: boil or for salads
Features: long and oval with very red skin and bright yellow, very tasty flesh. Loses its colour when cooked.

Dunbar Rover
Early
Origin: Scotland, 1936
Availability: Scotland (in small quantities and for local consumption)
Uses: boil
Features: oval to round with white skin and flesh and shallow eyes. Holds together when cooked.
(Photo p.59)

Dunbar Standard
Mid-season to late
Origin: Scotland, 1936
Availability: Ireland and United Kingdom
Uses: suitable for all types of cooking
Features: round or oval with white skin and flesh. Very tasty and firm.
(Photo p.59)

Duke of York

Dundrod
Very early (lift in April)
Origin: Northern Ireland, 1987
Availability: Canada, Holland, Northern Ireland, Sweden and United Kingdom
Uses: boil, for chips and purée
Features: round to oval with bright yellow skin and white, firm and creamy flesh. Widely used for making fish and chips.

Dunluce
Very early
Origin: Northern Ireland, 1976
Uses: suitable for all types of cooking
Features: round, with firm, white skin and flesh, shallow eyes.

Dunluce

Duke of York Red

Foremost (x 2) | Home Guard (p. 58) | Epicure | Lady Chrystal (p. 61)

Edgecote Purple
Mid-season to early
Origin: United Kingdom, 1916
Availability: collectors' potato only
Features: long and oval with white skin and bright yellow flesh.

Edzell Blue
Early
Origin: Scotland, before 1915
Availability: Scotland
Uses: boil and purée
Features: round with blue skin and shiny white, floury, tasty flesh. Its eyes are very deep. Boil it with care because it bursts easily. Very good steamed or microwaved.
(Photo p.58)

Eigenheimer
Mid-season to early
Origin: Holland, 1893
Availability: Holland, Zaïre
Uses: fry and for chips
Features: oval with white skin and yellow flesh. Very good for chips.

Elvira
Origin: unknown
Availability: Italy
Uses: boil and for chips
Features: faintly oval with firm, yellow skin and flesh and deep eyes.

Epicure
Very early (lift in April)
Origin: United Kingdom, 1897
Availability: Canada and United Kingdom
Uses: boil and bake
Features: round with white skin and white, cracked, firm flesh and very deep eyes. Has a very distinctive flavour.

Estima
Early
Origin: Holland, 1973
Availability: Algeria and Northern Europe
Uses: boil, bake, roast and for chips
Features: oval and uniform, with bright yellow skin and watery, firm flesh. Cream-coloured with shallow eyes.

Fianna
Very early
Origin: Holland, 1987
Availability: Holland, New Zealand and United Kingdom
Uses: bake, purée, roast or for chips
Features: smooth with white skin and firm, floury flesh. Very tasty.

Foremost
Very early
Origin: United Kingdom, 1954
Features: round to oval with firm, white skin and flesh and shallow eyes. First known as Sutton's Foremost, it was a favourite with gardeners for many years, both for its flavour and for its cooking potential.

Forty Fold
Very early
Origin: United Kingdom, 1893
Availability: United Kingdom (very limited)
Uses: suitable for all types of cooking
Features: irregular-shaped tubers with white or brilliant purple skin, reddish or white markings and very deep eyes. Its flesh is creamy and tasty.

Franceline
Origin: France, 1993
Availability: France
Uses: suitable for all types of cooking
Features: long tuber with light pink skin and firm but tender flesh.

Franceline

Edgecote Purple

Maris Peer (p. 61) | Fingerlin | Estima | Linzer Delikatess (p. 61) | Osprey (p. 62)

Forty Fold

Francine
Mid-season to early
Origin: France, 1993
Availability: France, Germany and United Kingdom
Uses: boil or in salads
Features: red skin and pearly white flesh, very soft and firmish. Has a very distinctive flavour.

Frisia
Very early
Origin: Holland
Availability: Bulgaria, Canada, Europe and New Zealand
Uses: boil, bake, roast or for salads
Features: oval, with yellow skin and white, damp flesh, slightly firm and creamy.

Gemchip
Mid-season to late
Origin: United States, 1989
Availability: Canada, United States (Colorado, Idaho, Oregon, Washington)
Uses: boil, bake, purée and for chips
Features: small and round with smooth, light skin and white flesh.

Golden Wonder
Semi-late to late
Origin: United Kingdom, 1906
Availability: United Kingdom
Uses: boil, roast, purée or for chips
Features: wide and oval with reddish brown skin and white, very floury flesh but tasty when cooked. Excellent for making chips. Its flavour improves on keeping for a few days.

Edzell Blue (p. 56)

Goldrush
Mid-season to early
Origin: United States (North Dakota), 1992
Availability: Canada, United States
Uses: boil, bake or roast. Quite good for other types of cooking
Features: oblong, with light brown skin and very white, tasty flesh. New variety of red potato.

Granola
Early to very early
Origin: Germany, 1975
Availability: Australia, Germany, Holland, India, Indonesia, Pakistan, Turkey and Vietnam
Uses: boil, bake or for chips
Features: oval with bright yellow skin and creamy, yellow flesh.

Harmony
Early to very early
Origin: Scotland, 1998
Features: very smooth, firm and white.

Home Guard
Very early (lift in April)
Origin: Scotland, 1942
Availability: United Kingdom
Uses: boil, roast, for chips. Suitable for all other types of cooking
Features: round or oval with white skin and pearly white, floury flesh. Its flavour is slightly bitter. High dry-matter content.

Ilam Hardie
All year round
Origin: unknown
Availability: South Africa and New Zealand
Uses: boil, bake, roast, purée, for chips or salads
Features: yellow skin and white, floury, tasty flesh.

International Kidney, Jersey Royal
Early to very early
Origin: United Kingdom, 1879
Availability: Australia, Europe and United Kingdom
Uses: boil or for salads
Features: long and oval with flaky white and yellow skin. Its flesh is pale yellow and firm with a delicious buttery flavour.

Irish Cobbler, America
Very early (lift in April)
Origin: United States, 1876
Availability: Canada, South Korea and United States
Uses: boil, purée or for chips
Features: round and white, medium to large. Its skin is white, cracked and smooth.

Itasca
Mid-season to early
Origin: Minnesota, 1994
Availability: Canada and United States
Uses: boil, bake, roast, purée or for chips
Features: oblong to round, with smooth, pale skin. Its flesh is white and cracked.

Jaerla
Very early (lift in April)
Origin: Holland, 1969
Availability: Algeria, Argentina, Greece, Holland, Spain, Turkey and Yugoslavia
Uses: boil, bake and suitable for all other types of cooking
Features: long, slightly oval with bright yellow, firm flesh.

Kanona
Mid-season to early
Origin: United States, 1989
Availability: Canada and United States
Uses: boil, bake, purée and for chips
Features: round and fat with white, slightly mottled skin and flesh.

Karlena
Origin: West Germany, 1993
Availability: Egypt, France, Germany, Hungary, Israel, Scandinavia, United Kingdom
Uses: purée, roast or for chips
Features: round, medium-sized with yellow skin and golden-yellow, floury flesh.

Katahdin
Mid-season to late
Origin: United States, 1932
Availability: Canada, New Zealand, United States
Uses: boil, bake, for salads and all other types of cooking
Features: round to oval, has smooth, fine skin and white, firm flesh. Watery.

Kondor (p. 60) Romano (p. 65)
Dunbar Standard (p. 54) Harmony

King Edward and Red (p. 60) Dunbar Rover (p. 54)
Majestic (p. 61) Record (p. 65)

Kennebec

Mid-season to early
Origin: United States, 1948
Availability: Argentina, Australia, Canada, Italy, New Zealand, Portugal, South Korea, Taiwan, United States, Uruguay
Uses: boil, bake, for chips, purée or roast
Features: oval to round, with very smooth skin and white flesh. This is the variety favoured by gardeners in the United States.

Kepplestone Kidney

Early to very early
Origin: United Kingdom, 1919
Availability: not sold
Uses: boil
Features: blue skin and yellow flesh with a very rich, buttery flavour.

Kerr's Pink

Mid-season to late
Origin: Scotland, 1917
Availability: Holland, Ireland, United Kingdom
Uses: boil, bake, purée, roast or for chips
Features: round with partially pink skin and cream, floury flesh with very deep eyes. Good flavour.

Kestrel

Early
Origin: Scotland, 1992
Availability: United Kingdom
Features: long, with white-blue skin and cream, slightly firm flesh, with shallow eyes. Loses its colour when cooked.

Kestrel

King Edward and Red

Mid-season to early
Origin: United Kingdom, 1902
Availability: Australia, Canaries, New Zealand, Portugal, Spain, United Kingdom
Uses: bake, purée, roast, for chips or other methods
Features: bean-shaped, oval with pink skin, slightly dark at the ends and with floury, pale yellow to cream flesh. The most popular potato in Great Britain in the 20th century.
(Photo p.59)

Kondor

Early
Origin: Holland, 1984
Uses: suitable for all types of cooking
Features: long, with red skin, firm, yellow flesh and quite dark eyes.
(Photo p.59)

Lady Crystal

Maris Peer

Lady Crystal
Very early
Origin: Holland, 1996
Uses: boil and steam
Features: long, with yellow skin, soft, dark yellow flesh and shallow eyes.
(Photo p.56)

Lewis Black
Very early
Origin: United Kingdom
Availability: United Kingdom
Features: long and oval with blue skin, white flesh and surface eyes

Linzer Delikatess
Early
Origin: Austria, 1976
Availability: Austria, France, United Kingdom
Uses: boil, excellent in salads
Features: oval, pear-shaped with pale yellow skin and firm, yellow flesh. Flavour similar to Ratte potatoes.
(Photo p.57)

Majestic
Very early
Origin: Scotland, 1911
Availability: Italy, United Kingdom
Uses: boil, bake, purée
Features: oval, longish with white skin and flesh and a sweetish flavour. Although previously the most cultivated variety in Great Britain, it has lost its place in the market but continues to be grown by amateur gardeners. Prefers dry conditions.
(Photo p.59)

Maori Chief, Peru
Early
Origin: New Zealand
Availability: New Zealand
Uses: boil, roast or for salads
Features: black and purple skin and flesh. Does not need peeling. Very good sweet flavour when steamed. Best consumed in 10 days once lifted.

Marfona
Early
Origin: Holland, 1975
Availability: Cyprus, Greece, Holland, Israel, Portugal, Turkey, United Kingdom
Uses: boil, bake, purée or for chips
Features: round to oval with light beige to yellow skin, soft, firm flesh and a mildly peppery flavour.

Lewis Black

Maris Bard
Very early (lift in April)
Origin: United Kingdom, 1972
Availability: United Kingdom
Uses: boil and suitable for all cooking types
Features: white skin and white, firm, cracked flesh with a distinctive flavour. It is one of the earliest potatoes known. If kept, it sometimes collapses when cooked and loses its flavour.
(Photo p.69)

Maris Peer
Early
Origin: United Kingdom, 1962
Availability: United Kingdom
Uses: boil, for chips and salads
Features: oval to round with firm, cream skin and flesh and shallow eyes. Keeps its colour but does not have a very interesting flavour.
(Photo p.57)

Maris Piper
Very early
Origin: United Kingdom, 1964
Availability: Portugal, United Kingdom
Uses: bake, purée, roast or for chips
Features: oval with creamy, floury, tasty skin and flesh. Very famous in Great Britain for making fish and chips. Splits open if reheated.

Maxine
Very early
Origin: Scotland, 1993
Features: oval with red skin and firm, creamy flesh and shallow eyes. Loses its colour when cooked and is quick to collapse.

Mona Lisa
Early
Origin: Holland, 1982
Availability: France, Greece, Holland and Portugal
Uses: boil, bake, purée, roast or for chips
Features: long and oval, bean-shaped with yellow skin and flesh and a firm texture that turns floury once cooked. Tastes of fresh nuts.
(Photo p.67)

Mondial
Very early
Origin: Holland, 1987
Availability: Greece, Holland, Israel and New Zealand
Uses: bake, purée, roast or for chips
Features: long and oval with yellow, floury skin and flesh.

Maris Piper | Pentland Crown | Navan

Midas
Very early
Origin: United Kingdom, 1996
Features: oval with white skin, cream, very floury skin and shallow eyes.
(Photo p.69)

Mimi
Very early
Origin: United Kingdom
Availability: United Kingdom
Features: red skin.

Monona
Very early
Origin: United States, 1964
Availability: Canada, United States (mid-north and north-east States)
Uses: boil, bake and for chips
Features: oval to round with chamois-white skin.

Navan
Early to mid-season
Origin: Northern Ireland, 1987
Availability: Ireland, United Kingdom
Features: oval with white skin and cracked white, rather floury flesh and shallow eyes.

Nicola
Early and all year
Origin: West Germany, 1973
Availability: Australia, Austria, Cyprus, Egypt, France, Germany, Israel, Morocco, New Zealand, Portugal, Switzerland, Tunisia, United Kingdom
Uses: boil, bake, purée, roast, for chips and in salads
Features: long and oval with yellow skin and dark, firm yellow flesh. Excellent buttery flavour. First cultivated around the Mediterranean basin, it has now acquired world-wide popularity for use in salads.

Old Black
Late
Origin: United Kingdom before 1951
Availability: United Kingdom
Features: oval to round with partially blue skin and white flesh with blue rings.

Orla
Very early
Origin: Ireland, United Kingdom, 1978
Availability: Ireland, United Kingdom
Uses: boil, fry
Features: long and oval with white skin, yellow flesh and surface eyes.

Osprey
Early
Origin: Scotland, 1999
Uses: boil, bake and suitable for all types of cooking
Features: oval with pinkish-white skin and white, cracked, soft flesh with shallow eyes.
(Photo p.57)

Othello
Very early
Origin: Scotland, 1996
Features: oval with white and red skin, cream, very firm flesh and shallow eyes.

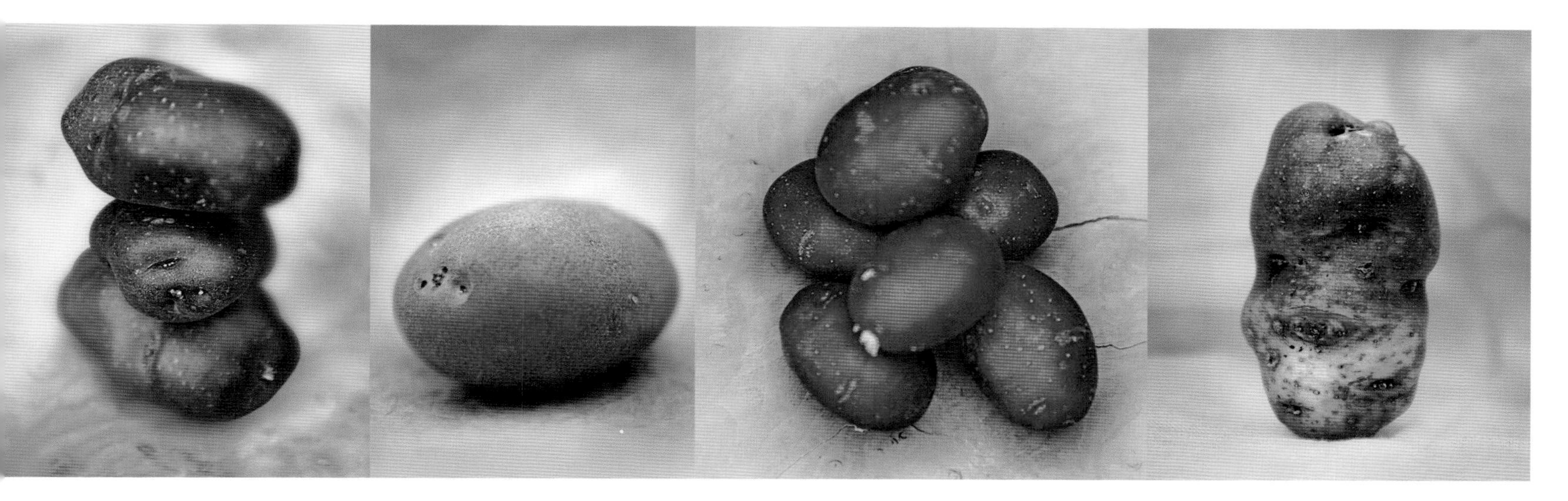

Orkney Black Maxine Mimi Old Black

Penta

Early
Origin: Holland, 1983
Availability: Canada, Holland
Uses: boil, bake, purée or roast
Features: round with cream skin, very deep eyes and pink to red flesh. The flesh has a very creamy texture and breaks up when boiled. Excellent when steamed or microwaved.

Pentland Crown

Mid-season to early
Origin: Scotland, 1959
Availability: Malawi, United Kingdom (very rare)
Uses: boil, bake or roast
Features: oval to round with white skin and cracked white flesh. The first of the Penta variety to gain popularity in the 1970s, especially in eastern England.

Pentland Dell

Very early
Origin: Scotland, 1961
Availability: New Zealand, South Africa, United Kingdom
Uses: bake, purée, roast or for chips
Features: medium-sized, long and thin, with white skin and cracked white flesh. Dry texture, very good for purées.

Pentland Hawk

Very early
Origin: Scotland, 1966
Availability: United Kingdom
Uses: boil, bake, purée, roast or for chips
Features: oval with white skin and flesh. Creamy and very tasty. Very popular in Scotland. Keeps very well with a tendency to lose its colour once cooked.

Pentland Ivory

Very early
Origin: Scotland, 1966
Features: round, with cracked white skin and flesh. Floury with shallow eyes.

Riviera (p. 65) Pentland Javelin (x2) (p. 64) Othello (x2) Orla (p. 62)

Pentland Javelin

Very early
Origin: Scotland, 1966
Availability: United Kingdom
Uses: boil or in salads
Features: oval, medium-sized with white skin and flesh and very shallow eyes. A very good new potato, soft and floury.
(Photo p.63)

Picasso

Very early
Origin: Holland, 1992
Availability: Balearic Islands, Cyprus, Egypt, Holland, Portugal, Spain, United Kingdom
Uses: boil and in salads
Features: small, oval to round, pale skin and firm, white flesh with very deep red eyes.

Pink Eye, Southern Gold, Sweet Gold or Pink Gourmet

Early
Origin: United Kingdom, 1862
Availability: Australia
Uses: boil, purée, for salads and suitable for all types of cooking
Features: small and smooth with cream skin. Its flesh is purplish-blue and creamy yellow with a floury texture and a nutty flavour. Originally from Kent and now grown in Australia.

Pink Fair Apple

Mid-season to late
Origin: France, 1850
Availability: Australia, France, United Kingdom
Uses: boil, roast or for salads
Features: long and knobbly with light pink skin and pink or yellowish blue patches. Its eyes are very deep and the flesh firm with a delicious flavour of fresh nuts. Best cooked with its skin. Difficult to peel raw.

Pompadour

Very early
Origin: Holland, 1976
Availability: France
Uses: boil, steam or for salads
Features: long, oval and regular, with light yellow skin and flesh.

Pink Fair Apple/Robinta/Rooster (p. 66)

Première
Very early (lift in April)
Origin: Holland, 1979
Availability: Bulgaria, Canada, Holland, United Kingdom
Uses: boil, bake, roast or for chips
Features: oval and wide with pale yellow skin and flesh. Good flavour.

Ratte, Cornichon or Princess
Mid-season
Origin: France, 1872
Availability: Australia, Denmark, France, Germany, United Kingdom
Uses: boil, purée or in salads
Features: long, tubular, looks like a small banana, less knobbly than the Pink Fair Apple. Yellowish brown skin and cream flesh with a firm texture and delicious flavour of hazelnuts. Popularised in France by star chef Joël Robuchon's purée.

Record
Very early
Origin: Holland, 1932
Availability: Greece, Holland, Yugoslavia, United Kingdom
Uses: bake, purée, roast or for chips
Features: white skin with pink nuances and yellow flesh. Floury texture and great flavour. Good for all types of cooking and excellent puréed.
(Photo p.59)

Red Drayton
Mid-season
Origin: Great Britain, 1976
Availability: Holland and Great Britain
Uses: bake, roast or for chips
Features: round, medium-sized with red and white skin and white flesh.
(Photo p.66)

Red Rooster
Very early
Origin: Ireland, 1993
Availability: Ireland
Uses: boil, bake, purée, roast and for chips or salads
Features: flat and oval, with shiny red skin and firm yellow flesh. Mild flavour. Can be used as a new potato.

Red Ruby
Mid-season to early
Origin: United States, 1994
Availability: Canada, United States
Uses: boil and bake
Features: oblong, with dark red skin, brown patches and shiny white flesh. Very good for winter consumption.

Rioja
Very early
Origin: Hungary, 1999
Availability: United Kingdom
Uses: bake or for chips
Features: oval with red skin, pale yellow flesh and a very floury texture.

Riviera
Very early
Origin: Holland, 1999
Uses: boil, bake or for salads
Features: oval with yellow skin and dark cream, firmish flesh with shallow eyes.
(Photo p.63)

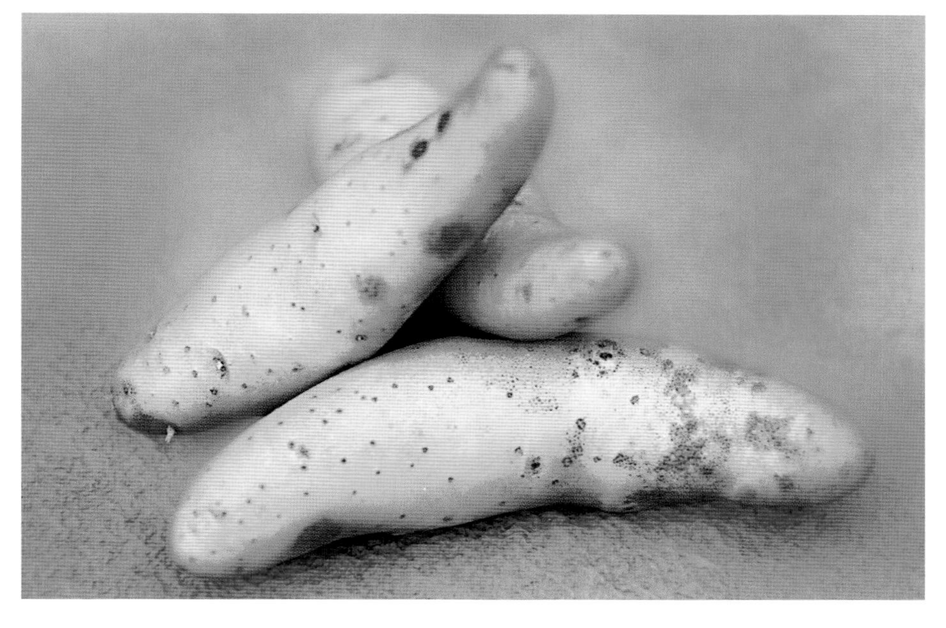

Ratte

Robinta
Very early
Origin: Holland, 1992
Features: oval with red skin and white, rather floury flesh and shallow eyes.

Rocket
Very early (lift in April)
Origin: United Kingdom, 1987
Availability: New Zealand, United Kingdom
Uses: boil, bake, purée, roast or for chips or salads
Features: round and uniform with white skin and flesh. Very tasty new potato with a firm texture.

Rode Pipo
Mid-season
Origin: Holland, 1982
Availability: Holland and United Kingdom
Features: oval, with red skin, yellow flesh and surface eyes.
(Photo p.66)

Romano
Very early
Origin: Holland, 1978
Availability: Balearic Islands, Cameroon, Holland, Hungary, Portugal, Spain, United Kingdom
Uses: boil, bake, purée or roast
Features: round to oval with red skin, soft, creamy flesh and a pleasant flavour faintly reminiscent of hazelnuts. When cooked, it turns from red to beige.
(Photo p.59)

Rode Pipo (p. 65)

Royal Kidney

Early
Origin: United Kingdom
Availability: Majorca, United Kingdom
Uses: for salads
Features: bean-shaped with soft white skin and firm, pale yellow flesh.

Red Drayton (p. 65)

Rioja (p. 65)

Romano (p. 65)

Rooster

Very early
Origin: Ireland, 1993
Uses: suitable for all types of cooking
Features: oval with red skin, pale yellow flesh and shallow eyes. Floury texture.
(Photo p.64)

Rosabelle

Early
Origin: France, 1978
Availability: France and United Kingdom
Features: long and oval with red skin, yellow flesh and shallow eyes.

Roseval

Very early
Origin: France, 1950
Availability: Australia, France, Israel, New Zealand, United Kingdom
Uses: boil, microwave or for salads
Features: oval with dark red-purplish skin and firm, golden flesh. Delicious buttery flavour.

Rosine

Very early
Origin: Brittany, 1972
Availability: France
Uses: boil, for gratins or salads. Very good steamed
Features: red skin and cracked pink skin. Descended from the BF15 and Roseval. Excellent flavour and a good keeper.

Russet Burbank, Idaho Russet or Netted Gem

Mid-season to late
Origin: United States, 1875
Availability: Australia, Canada, New Zealand, United States (Central North-East and Mid-West States), United Kingdom
Uses: purée or roast. Excellent for chips
Features: long and oval with reddish to brown skin and pale yellow to white, floury, tasty flesh. Very deep eyes. Turns shiny on cooking. This potato originates from Idaho and is very popular in the United States. Adopted by McDonald's.

Saxon (p. 69) | Mona Lisa (p. 62) | Swift (p. 69) | Yukon Gold (p. 71)

Salad Blue

Origin: United States
Availability: United States and United Kingdom
Features: short and oval with blue skin and light purplish-blue flesh. Deepish eyes.
(Photo p.69)

Salad Red

Origin: United Kingdom
Availability: United Kingdom
Features: long and oval with red skin, pinkish-red flesh and surface eyes.
(Photo p.69)

Roseval | Stroma (p. 69) | Rosabelle | Ulster Chieftain (p. 70)

Charlotte (p. 52)

Shetland Black

Samba
Very early
Origin: France, 1989
Availability: France, Portugal, Spain
Uses: THE potato for every type of cooking!
Features: oval and regular with white skin and yellow, floury flesh.

Sante
Early to very early
Origin: Holland, 1983
Availability: Bulgaria, Canada, Holland, United Kingdom
Uses: boil, bake, roast or for chips
Features: round to oval with white to light yellow skin and flesh. Has a dry, firm texture with deepish eyes. This variety has become the most popular of the organic potatoes.

Saxon
Early
Origin: United Kingdom, 1992
Availability: United Kingdom (still rare)
Uses: boil, bake and for chips
Features: white skin and firm, damp flesh. Excellent flavour. Very popular, sold in sacks in markets.
(Photo p.67)

Sharpe's Express
Very early to early
Origin: United Kingdom, 1900
Availability: occasionally available in Scotland
Uses: boil (very fragile), bake, purée and roast
Features: shaped like an oval pear with white skin, cream rather floury flesh and shallow eyes. Needs to be boiled with care and loses some of its colour.

Shetland Black or Black Kidney
Early
Origin: United Kingdom, 1923
Availability: United Kingdom (very limited)
Uses: boil and purée
Features: blue-black skin and yellow flesh with a single purple ring on the inside. Very feathery and floury with an exceptionally sweet, buttery flavour. Turns grey-blue when puréed. Hint: if you want to keep the bluish colour, cook it in the oven before mashing.

Skerry Blue
Mid-season to late
Origin: United Kingdom, 1846
Availability: United Kingdom (rare)
Uses: boil
Features: purple skin and mottled, dark purple and white or cream flesh. Has a superb flavour.

Salad Blue (p. 67)

Salad Red (p. 67)

Stemster
Very early
Origin: Scotland
Uses: suitable for all types of cooking
Features: oval with red skin, golden yellow, firmish flesh and deep eyes.

Stroma
Early
Origin: Scotland, 1989
Availability: United Kingdom
Features: long and oval with red skin and firm, yellow flesh with a delicate flavour. Deepish eyes.
(Photo p.67)

Sweet Potato
Mid-season to early
Origin: South America
Availability: Japan, Pacific Islands, Russia, United States (Southern States)
Uses: boil, bake, purée and roast. Suitable for all types of cooking.
Features: there are two varieties of Sweet Potato, one with white skin, the other with reddish-brown skin. The reddish-brown variety is sweeter and firmer. The Sweet Potato is different from the potato because its tuber comes from a tropical creeper. It has the same features: the edible part is the tuber, the skin and flesh come in various colours and can be treated like the potato.

Swift
Very early
Origin: Scotland, 1994
Uses: suitable for all types of cooking
Features: oval with white skin, soft, golden yellow flesh and shallow eyes.

Spey
Very early
Origin: Scotland, 1997
Uses: suitable for all types of cooking
Features: long with red and white skin, soft, cream flesh and shallow eyes.

Spunta
Early
Origin: Holland, 1968
Availability: Argentina, Australia, Cyprus, Greece, Holland, Indonesia, Italy, Malaysia, Mauritius, New Zealand, Portugal, Thailand, Tunisia, United Kingdom, Vietnam.
Uses: boil, bake, purée, roast or for chips or salads
Features: bean- or pear-shaped, medium-sized to large, long with yellow skin and golden flesh.

Stemster | Spey
Valor (p. 70) | Midas (p. 62)

Maris Bard (p. 61) | Ulster Sceptre (p. 70)
Sharpe's Express | Sante

Vanessa

Triumph Red Bliss

Yetholm Gipsy

Thomes
Early
Origin: Ireland, before 1924
Availability: Ireland, United Kingdom
Features: long and oval with blue skin and white flesh.

Triumph Red Bliss
Late
Origin: United Kingdom, 1982
Availability: United Kingdom
Features: round with white skin and flesh.

Ulster Chieftain
Very early
Origin: Northern Ireland, 1938
Features: oval with fragile, white skin and flesh and deep eyes. Breaks up when cooked. Can be grown indoors.
(Photo p.67)

Ulster Sceptre
Very early
Origin: Northern Ireland, 1963
Availability: Northern Ireland
Uses: suitable for all types of cooking
Features: small and oval with white and yellow skin, cracked, white flesh and shallow eyes. Has a firmish texture. Sometimes darkens when cooked.
(Photo p.69)

Valor
Very early
Origin: Scotland, 1993
Availability: Canaries, Israel, United Kingdom
Uses: boil or bake
Features: oval with white skin and cracked, white flesh.
(Photo p.69)

Vanessa
Very early
Origin: Holland, 1973
Availability: Holland and United Kingdom
Uses: boil, roast or in salads
Features: long and oval with pink and red skin, soft, bright yellow flesh and shallow eyes.

Verity
Mid-season to late
Origin: Scotland, 1998
Availability: United Kingdom
Uses: very good roasted
Features: oval with white skin, cracked, white, floury flesh and shallow eyes.

Vitelotte or Truffe de Chine
Very late
Origin: unknown
Availability: France, United Kingdom (very rare)
Uses: boil, fry, purée, for chips or in salads.
Features: small, long and thin with purplish skin and mauve, firm, floury flesh that tastes faintly of hazelnuts. Turns 'bleu de Chine' (the colour of Chinese porcelain) when cooked. In France, the name 'Truffe de Chine' is not often used to avoid confusion with truffes chinoises.

White Lady
Mid-season to late
Origin: Hungary, 1999
Uses: suitable for all types of cooking
Features: oval with white skin, cracked, white, floury flesh and deep eyes.

Wilja
Early
Origin: Holland, 1967
Availability: Holland, Pakistan
Uses: boil, bake, purée, roast or for chips
Features: long and oval with bright yellow skin and flesh. Soft and dryish with shallow eyes.

Verity (x2)
White Lady (x2)

Verity

Winston

Wilja

Thomes

Yam

Winston

Very early (lift in April)
Origin: Scotland, 1992
Availability: New Zealand, United Kingdom
Uses: bake, roast, for chips or in salads
Features: uniformly oval with creamy white skin and very firm flesh.

Yam

Mid-season to late
Origin: Unknown, 1771
Uses: unremarkable
Features: oval to knobbly with pink and red skin and white flesh with pink patches.

Yetholm Gipsy

Origin: United Kingdom
Availability: United Kingdom
Features: oval with purplish-blue skin, white to cream flesh and shallow eyes.

Yukon Gold

Early to very early
Origin: Canada (Ontario), 1980
Availability: Canada and United States (California and Michigan)
Uses: boil, bake or for chips
Features: oval to round, large, with chamois-coloured skin, yellow, floury flesh and pink eyes. Cooking brings out a delicious flavour. Probably the most popular potato in the United States.
(Photo p.67)

10 Essential Potatoes

10 varieties for all types of cooking

Boil
Bake
For chips
Fry
Mash
Sauté
Roast

Fry
Mash

Bake
Sauté
For salads
Steam

For salads
Steam
Sauté
For stews
Mash
For mousses

Mash
Fry
Stew
For chips
Sauté
… all cooking methods

Boil
Bake
Mash
For chips
Fry
Roast

Skin
Agria

Skin
Vitelotte dite "la tru

Skin
Roseval

Skin
Ratte

Skin
Franceline

Skin
Mona Lisa

(This colour chart was designed by Pied à Coulisses)

potato colours

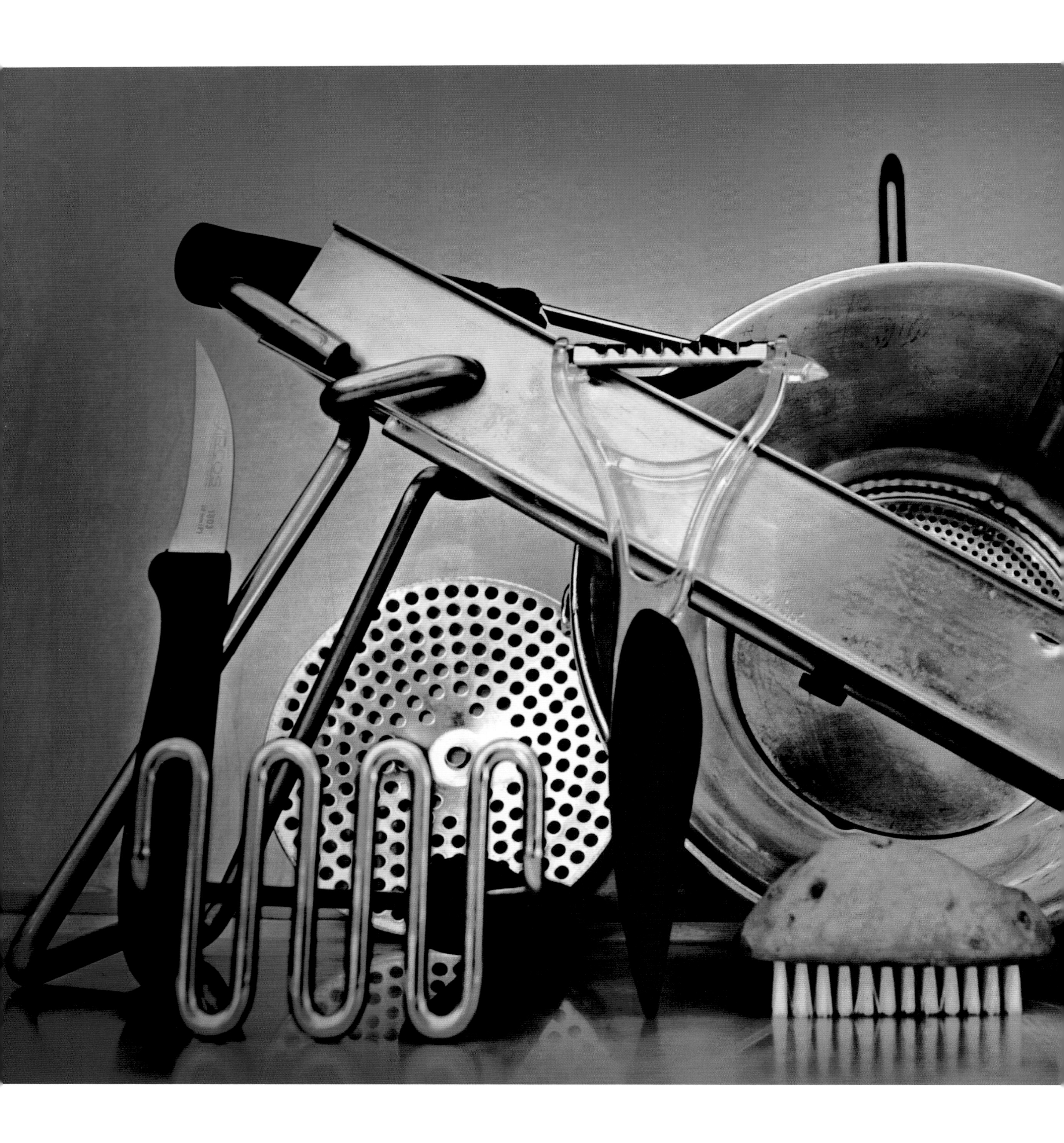

53 Potato Fanatics

Vitelotte Crisps with Old Mimolette

Éric has an artist's sense of colour and his 'Vitelotte Crisps with Old Mimolette' is a feast for the eyes.

Éric Frechon [Paris, France]

1

Cut the Vitelotte potatoes with their skins into slices 0.75cm thick using a slicing machine (slice them very finely by hand if you do not have one).

2

Put the potato slices to soak in salted water for 7 minutes.

3

Sponge off the crisps, fry at 160°C, then arrange them on a baking tray, sprinkle with pieces of Old Mimolette and put in the oven at 180°C for 2 minutes.

4

Put little pieces of Old Mimolette in a glass dish or bowl, arrange the crisps, then serve.

Wine suggestion: Vin Jaune (Pierre Overnoy).

Serves 4

- 250g Vitelotte potatoes
- 60g Old Mimolette
- 3 litres peanut oil

Latkes

Bintje galettes with onions

Nach Waxman [New York, US]

In New York, Nach opened the world's most important gastronomic bookshop - except for the Librairie Gourmande in Paris. His Latkes have been passed down through successive generations of the family by word of mouth, and he was eager to see them published.

1

Grate the Bintjes coarsely and leave them unpeeled. Set aside in a bowl for 30-40 minutes. (The potatoes will release some of the water and oxidise.)

2

Grate the onion coarsely and set aside.

3

Drain the grated potatoes and rinse under cold water for a few minutes. Press them gently between your hands and put in a bowl and set aside.

4

If the onions made a lot of juice, keep half the liquid and mix the onions with the potatoes. Add the eggs, flour, baking powder, salt and pepper and mix everything thoroughly.

5

Put 3mm corn oil in a high-sided frying pan. Heat the oil over a high heat for 3-4 minutes. Take a little of the batter in a slotted ladle and place in the pan. Brown the Latkes well on both sides and sponge off the excess oil by laying them on paper towels.

6

Serve the Latkes hot with apple purée or sour cream.

Wine suggestion: Medium dry Champagne.

Serves 4

- 6 big Bintje potatoes
- 1 medium-sized onion
- 2 eggs, lightly beaten
- 3 tablespoons flour
- $^{1}/_{2}$ teaspoon baking powder
- salt
- pepper
- corn oil for frying

Potato Macaire with Black Sausage

1

Wash and peel the Ratte potatoes. Cook them in lightly salted water for 20-25 minutes. Drain and purée in a vegetable mill. Work in the butter cut into small pieces and season with salt, pepper and Espelette pepper or chilli powder. Set aside at room temperature.

2

Remove the skin from the sausage and cut into slices 5mm thick.

Yves Camdeborde [Paris, France]

'Small cheer and great welcome makes a merry feast.'
Shakespeare in literature, Camdeborde in real life.

Serves 4

- 300g Ratte potatoes
- 500g black sausage
- 100g butter
- salt and pepper
- Espelette pepper (mild chilli)
- 1 apple

3

Arrange the sausage slices in neatly overlapping concentric circles in non-stick fan moulds (2cm high and 8cm across). Cover with the potato purée. Bake in a very hot oven for 12-15 minutes.

4

Turn out the pomme macaire on to a plate and serve with a seasonal salad with some of the apple.

Wine suggestion: Béarn 2001, Domaine Guilhemas (Pascal Lafeyre).

Spring Vegetable Salad

Thomas Keller [Yountville, US]

Before he would let us into his kitchen, Thomas showed us his garden - as amazing as his culinary creations.

1

Boil the chicken stock, stir in the butter and season with salt and pepper, add the peeled Ratte potatoes, the bay leaf and the garlic. Leave to simmer.

2

Cut the potatoes diagonally and add in the vegetables cut into small chunks to cook.

3

Arrange the vegetables and potatoes on a plate. Scatter the flowers and lettuce around the plate and drizzle with the vinaigrette.

Wine suggestion: Fumé Blanc 2000, Tokalon Vineyard-1-block (Robert Mondavi).

Serves 4

Ratte potatoes cooked in emulsified butter
- 8 Ratte potatoes
- 20g butter
- 1/2 litre chicken stock
- 1 bay leaf
- 1 tablespoon spring garlic
- salt and black pepper

Vegetables
- 4 green onions
- 4 bulbs garlic
- 8 wild leeks
- 12 wild asparagus spears

- 18 edible flowers (pansies, nasturtiums, garlic flowers) and baby lettuce

Vinaigrette
- 4 tablespoons olive oil
- 4 tablespoons balsamic vinegar

Spicy Pork Pot-au-Feu

Serves 6

- 1 large lightly salted knuckle of pork
- 1 lightly salted shoulder
- 1 lightly salted spare rib
- 3 pigs' tails
- 3 pigs' ears
- 1 leek
- 2 carrots
- 2 onions
- 1 head of garlic
- 4 large sweet potatoes
- 6 fennel bulbs
- 2 cloves
- 5 juniper berries
- 1 stick cinnamon
- 2 star anis
- 3 pinches saffron
- 1 litre dry white wine
- cornichons and pickled onions
- 50g grated horseradish
- coarse sea salt and peppercorns

Christophe Beaufront [Paris, France]

The sweet potato crept into this book without our intending to; Christophe's pot-au-feu was too good to miss.

1

In a casserole dish, put the knuckle of pork, the shoulder, spare rib, pigs' tails and ears. Cover with cold water and cook.

2

Add the garnish consisting of large chunks of leeks, carrots and onions, the garlic, spices and white wine. Leave to cook for about 2 hours (the meat should be tender).

3

An hour before the end of the cooking process, take off part of the liquid and use it to cook the peeled sweet potatoes and fennel.

4

Serve accompanied with the grated horseradish, cornichons, pickled onions and coarse salt.

Wine suggestion: Vouvray 2001 (Champalou).

Stuffed Bintjes Potatoes

Serves 4

- 100g minced beef
- 40g minced pork
- 20g minced jambon cru
- 4 slices jambon cru
- 8 firm, regular-shaped Bintje potatoes of medium size (7-8cm long and 5cm across)
- 3 échalotes grises
- 1/2 bunch parsley
- salt
- pepper
- goose or duck fat
- chicken stock

1

Make the stuffing with minced meat, very finely chopped shallots and minced parsley. Season with salt and pepper.

2

Peel the potatoes making them a regular, oval shape as you go. Use the peeler to scoop out the centre to leave a shell with sides 8mm thick.

3

Insert a small chunk of ham fat at the bottom of each potato. Fill with the stuffing and close t with a strip of jambon cru tucking the ends between the stuffing and the potato.

4

Heat the duck or goose fat in a large saucepan. Brown the potatoes and set aside. Line the pa of ham and put in the potatoes. Moisten with a little stock and cook with the lid on for 30 mi heat. The potatoes should be soft.

'Serve with a salad.'

Wine suggestion: Saint-Pourçain, Domaine Gosbot-Barbara (Didier Barbara).

Bénédict Beaugé [Paris, France]

Bénédict, a 'four-seasons' writer-journalist who founded the magazine 'Miam-Miam', fax-machines his cooking. This culinary correspondence, first broadcast by fax and now on the Internet, proves that fat is good and useful.

Potato Cake

Raquel's dishes offer a wonderful mix of cultures. Here is her Parmentier from La Plata, her Shepherd's Pie de la Pampa, her Gaucho Gratin.

Raquel Carena [Argentina]

Serves 6

Potato purée
- 1kg Bintje potatoes
- 100g butter
- 2 glasses of milk

Stuffing
- 750g finely chopped raw beef
- 200g onions
- 4 very ripe tomatoes
- 100g raisins
- 1 bunch parsley
- 1 level teaspoon ground cumin
- 1 level teaspoon mild chilli
- 70g pine kernels
- 1 egg yolk
- salt and pepper
- 3 tablespoons peanut oil
- 1 stick cinnamon

1

Purée: make the purée with the Bintje potatoes, milk and butter.

2

Stuffing: in a heavy-bottomed saucepan, sweat the roughly chopped onions in the peanut oil. Add the meat and brown for 10 minutes over a high heat. Quarter the tomatoes, scoop out the insides and add them to the saucepan with the raisins, chopped parsley, the cumin, mild chilli and pine kernels (these should be dry-fried and browned first). Season with salt and pepper.

3

In a gratin dish, arrange half the potato purée, cover with the meat stuffing and finish with the remaining purée. Brush with the beaten egg yolk. Bake in the oven for 40 minutes at 180°C. Serve hot with a salad.

Variation: replace the first layer of potato purée with a purée of sweet potatoes.

Wine suggestion: Collioure 1999, La Panède, Domaine de la Tourbillo.

Bintje Potatoes Stuffed with Warm Cassava, White Asparagus Tips, Green Onions in Salmon and Herb Kebab with Soy Butter

Arnold Hanbuckers [Bruges, Belgium]

More of a coach than a chef, Arnold is obsessed with passing on his love of cooking to young people.

Serves 4

- 4 Bintje potatoes, weighing about 125g each
- 150g cassava
- 2 tablespoons liquid crème fraîche
- 24 white asparagus spears
- 150g salmon
- 4 green onions
- 2 tablespoons olive oil
- 1 small lovage leaf cut into quarters
- 4 small basil leaves
- 4 red orache leaves
- 4 Italian sorrel leaves
- 4 salad burnet leaves
- 4 nettle leaves
- 4 leaves lemon verbena
- 4 leaves tarragon
- 2 tablespoons clarified butter
- 2 teaspoons soy sauce
- salt and pepper

1

Boil the Bintje potatoes in their skins in salted water. Cut the potatoes in half lengthwise and use a melon baller to scoop out the centre. Sauté them in the clarified butter until they are golden brown on the hollowed-out side.

2

Peel the cassavas and cook them in salted water. Mash them to a purée with a little single cream. Keep it warm.

3

Peel the asparagus and cook them in salted water (they should be crunchy). Keep the heads warm.

4

Cut small escalopes of salmon, wrap them around the green onions and leave to marinate for an hour in olive oil.

5

Wash and dry the herbs. Put a leaf of each herb on a skewer.

6

Clarify the butter, strain it through muslin and add to warm soy sauce. Give the sauce a good stir before pouring it over the potato.

7

Half stuff the Bintje potatoes with the warm cassava purée, then stick the warmed asparagus heads into it. Arrange the green onions wrapped in salmon among the asparagus. Spear each potato with a herb kebab and pour over the soy butter.

Wine suggestion: Viura 2001, Rioja (Abel Mendoza).

Estouffade of Bintje Potatoes with Morel Mushrooms

Régis' territory lies between the Velay and Vivarais and he visits it each morning. Nowadays, morels have replaced boletus mushrooms - a good thing too!

Régis Marcon [Saint-Bonnet-Le-Froid, France]

Serves 6

- 120g dried morel mushrooms (prepare a day in advance)
- 1.5kg Bintje potatoes
- 3/4 litre chicken stock
- 100ml milk
- 250g crème fraîche
- 1 garlic clove, crushed
- 1 sprig thyme
- 70g butter
- 2 shallots, minced
- salt and pepper
- nutmeg

1

The day before: soak the morel mushrooms in the warm chicken stock.

2

Next day: drain the mushrooms. Boil the mushroom juices, then reduce by three quarters. Pour in the milk and crème fraîche. Add the crushed garlic and sprig of thyme. Season with salt and pepper and add a few gratings of nutmeg. Simmer to reduce the liquid and strain.

3

Chop the mushrooms coarsely. Heat 30g of butter in a frying pan and sweat the minced shallots. Add the chopped mushrooms and brown everything.

4

Cut the Bintje potatoes finely into 3mm-thick slices. In a buttered gratin dish, arrange the first layer of potatoes. Add the mushrooms and cover with a second layer of potatoes. Sprinkle each layer with a little salt.

5

Cover the potatoes with the mushroom cream. Bake in the oven at 160°C for 40-50 minutes. Serve piping hot.

Wine suggestion: White Saint-Joseph 2001, Domaine Le-Clos-Florentin.

Papillote of Duck Foie Gras and Roseval Potatoes with Chilli Peppers

Didier Oudill and Edgar Dhur [Paris, France]

Serves 4

- 1 foie gras, weighing 500g
- 4 Roseval potatoes
- 4 small green chilli peppers
- 1 bay leaf
- 12g salt
- pepper
- 100ml chicken stock
- 70ml red wine vinegar
- 120g lambs lettuce

Alone or together, Didier and Edgar continue to delight guests with the simplicity of their dishes after a double-act of more than twenty years.

1

Wash and peel the Roseval potatoes and cut them into discs 5mm thick. Finely mince the bay leaf and cut the green chilli peppers into thin slivers.

2

Remove the gall from the duck foie gras and season with salt and pepper.

3

Take a sheet of aluminium foil and cut a rectangle 40 x 60cm. On the first third of the sheet, lay the potato discs with the bay and slices of pepper spread over them, then place the whole foie gras on top.

4

Fold the foil over to make a parcel and pour in the chicken stock before sealing it so that no air can get in. Bake the parcel in the oven at 200°C for 25 minutes.

5

Carefully take the foie gras out of the parcel and cut it into slices 1cm thick. Sprinkle the vinegar over the potatoes.

6

Divide the lambs lettuce among the plates, lay potato discs on it with slices of foie gras on top and pour over the cooking juices.

Wine suggestion: Jurançon sec 2001, Cuvée Marie (Charles Hours).

Normandy Conger Eel with Charlotte Potato Conserve

Brigitte Rakoczy [Colombes, France]

Brigitte and Philippe, her husband, are an essential part of life with their excellent fish which is always on the menu.

Serves 4

- 560g conger eel, sliced (head-side up)
- 12 Charlotte potatoes (small ones)
- 40g onions
- 20g carrots
- 1 bouquet garni
- 1 bottle cider
- salt and pepper

Beurre manié
- 15g flour
- 15g butter

1

Place a knob of butter in a saucepan, add the onions, the sliced carrots and the bouquet garni and cook gently. Add the cider and leave to simmer for 15 minutes.

2

Place the slices of conger eel on top, pour a little water (enough to cover the fish) over it and leave to cook for 10 minutes. Mix in the Charlotte potatoes, first washed and peeled, season with salt and pepper and leave to cook for 20 minutes over a medium heat.

3

Place slices of the fish and its garnish in a dish and keep it on the heat. Cream the butter, then use a wooden spatula to mix in the flour. Gradually stir the beurre manié into the cooking juices, bring to the boil and cook for 5 minutes. Strain through a conical sieve.

4

To finish, place the fish on warmed plates, pour the sauce over it and add the garnish.

Wine suggestion: Saumur Blanc, Domaine Saint-Just 1997 (Yves Lambert).

Casserole of Baby Octopus with Ratte Potatoes and Garlic

Santi's cooking matches his personality: generous, insatiable, surprising and always refined.

Santi Santamaría [Sant-Celoni, Spain]

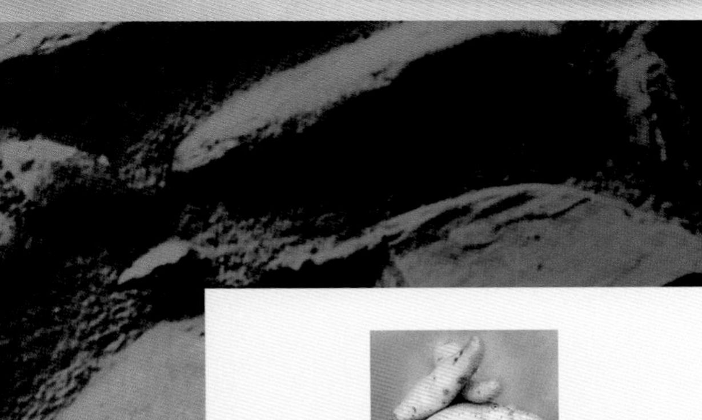

Serves 4

- 600g baby octopus
- 8 Ratte potatoes
- 1 head of garlic
- 5 strands saffron

For 1/4 litre vegetable nage
- 3 litres water
- 1/4 litre white wine
- 1/2 celery stalk
- 1 peeled carrot
- 1 courgette
- 1/2 fennel bulb
- 1 peeled onion
- 1 leek
- 1/2 bunch parsley
- 1 tablespoon black peppercorns
- salt
- olive oil

1

For the vegetable nage: chop the vegetables and put them in a saucepan with the cold water. Add the wine, black peppercorns and salt and simmer for 20 minutes. Sieve the nage and set aside.

2

Wash and peel the Ratte potatoes to make them cylindrical, then cut them into discs 0.5cm thick.

3

Put the potato discs to cook in a casserole dish with the vegetable nage and saffron for 20 minutes. Season with salt and pepper.

4

Cut the garlic in half and blanch it. Drain and sauté in the olive oil. Set aside.

5

Clean the baby octopus and sauté them in a little olive oil. Add the octopus and garlic to the casserole dish, cover and serve in a shallow bowl or in individual ramekins.

Wine suggestion: Pazo de Señorans, Selection Añada, 1999, Rias-Baixas.

My Cheesy Potato Purée

Mémé Bras [Laguiole, France]

'A smiling face is half the meal', says a Latvian proverb. Proof of the proverb is Mémé Bras.

1

Boil the Bintje potatoes in their skins in lightly salted water. Peel and purée them in the vegetable mill. Put the purée in a saucepan and add the butter in small chunks and the crème fraîche. Season with salt and pepper.

2

Heat the purée and add the finely sliced tomme. Mix with a wooden spatula, still on the heat. The tomme will gradually melt and combine with the purée. When the mixture is homogenous, adjust the seasoning as necessary and add a pinch of chopped garlic. Remove from the heat and bring the potato purée to the table piping hot.

'The ideal tomme should have matured for 2 to 4 days. To check the maturity spear a piece of tomme on the end of a fork and hold it over a flame for 30-40 seconds. Once hot, the tomme will run without breaking if it is ready for use.'

Wine suggestion: Vin Blanc Entraygues-le-Fel.

Serves 4-6

- 1kg Bintje potatoes
- 150g butter
- 150g crème fraîche
- 300-400g fresh tomme de Planèze
- salt
- pepper
- garlic

Sunday Roast Ratte Potatoes

Benoît Guichard [Paris, France]

Serves 4

- 800g small Ratte potatoes or small new Noirmoutier potatoes
- 6 cloves fresh garlic
- 1/2 bunch of small spring onions
- 2 slices smoked pork breast
- 1 heaped spoonful cool butter
- 1 drizzle peanut oil
- a few sprigs of fresh thyme and rosemary
- 3 spoonfuls good syrupy gravy (from roast veal, poultry or beef)
- fine salt

If, like us, you have the pleasure of welcoming great chefs to your table, then this recipe is for them… and for you!

1

Scrape the Ratte potatoes with a knife and wash and dry them. In a frying pan or high-sided frying pan (for sautéing), put a drizzle of oil and a good spoonful of butter. Heat the fat. Add the potatoes and unpeeled cloves of garlic, then the spring onions. Fry stirring frequently.

2

Three quarters of the way through the cooking process, add the slices of smoked pork in chunks and the thyme, rosemary and salt. Finish the cooking and allow to brown, stirring regularly.

3

Just before serving, sprinkle a few spoonfuls of the gravy over them, stirring continually over the heat for 2 or 3 minutes to glaze. Serve.

Wine suggestion: Côte-de-Beauve 1998, Domaine Michel-Gaunoux.

Charlotte Potatoes in a Salt Crust

Alain Passard [Paris, France]

'In cooking, as in every art, simplicity is a sign of perfection' (Curnonsky). Odd that he did not know this recipe...

Serves 4

- 8 Charlottes, weighing 100g each
- 4kg coarse sea salt from the Guérande
- 130g salted butter
- 400ml water
- 1 bunch flat parsley
- 1 sweet onion from the Cévennes
- fleur de sel
- olive oil

1

On a baking tray, make a base of coarse salt 4cm thick. Lay the potatoes on it evenly spaced and bury them in the remains of the coarse salt. Bake in the oven for 50 minutes at 150°C. When they are cooked, leave to stand for 30 minutes.

2

Meanwhile, remove the stalks from the flat parsley and boil the parsley in salted water for 3 minutes. Then transfer it to the blender bowl with 80g salted butter and 200ml of the cooking water from the parsley. Blend for 5 minutes, adjusting the seasoning with fine sea salt, then pour through a very fine-mesh sieve.

3

Peel the onion and slice very thinly. In a saucepan, melt 50g of the remaining butter and add the onion and 400ml water. Cook for 10 minutes over a low heat. Blend, adjust the seasoning and pour through a fine-mesh sieve.

4

Break the salt crust at the table and take out the potatoes. Peel them and mash them roughly with a fork two at a time, then with a tablespoon make potato dumplings. Pour the parsley coulis into the centre of each plate, then place a dumpling in it. Encircle with the onion fondue and decorate with a drizzle of olive oil.

Wine suggestion: Minervois Blanc 2001, Château La-Tour-Boisée (A. Marie-Claude).

The gratin dauphinois

Jeffrey Steingarten [New York, US]

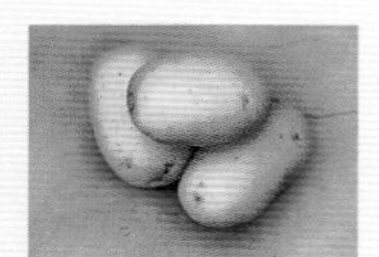

Serves 4

- 680g Belle de Fontenay potatoes
- 115g butter at room temperature
- 250ml milk
- 375ml crème fraîche
- 1 clove garlic, peeled
- salt
- white pepper
- grated nutmeg

Our friend Jeffrey Steingarten, food 'journalist, researcher and inspector', taught us a thing or two about French haute cuisine with this classic gratin dauphinois.

1

Bring the milk to the boil with the lightly crushed garlic clove, the salt, pepper and the nutmeg, and stir constantly. Remove from the heat and leave to infuse.

2

Meanwhile, peel and wash the Belle de Fontenay potatoes and wipe them on a tea towel. Cut them into 3mm-thick discs. Use half the butter to grease the base of a gratin dish and arrange the potato discs in it.

3

Bring the milk back to the boil, take out the garlic clove, then pour the milk over the potatoes and cover the gratin dish with a sheet of aluminium foil. Bake in the oven at 220°C for 15 minutes, or until the milk has been absorbed.

4

Bring the crème fraîche to the boil and pour over the gratin. Dice the rest of the butter and arrange on the top. Put in the oven without covering for 20-25 minutes until the potatoes turn golden brown.

Wine suggestion: Beaujolais Blanc 1999, Domaine des Terres-Dorées (J.-P. Brun).

Bharwanaloo
Tandoori Stuffed Potatoes

Vineet Bhatia [London, England]

Serves 4

- 4 medium-sized Franceline potatoes
- peanut oil for frying

Marinade
(prepare 4 hours in advance)
- 4 tablespoons thick yogurt
- 1 tablespoon ginger paste
- 1 teaspoon garlic paste
- 1/2 teaspoon ground turmeric
- 1/2 teaspoon red chilli powder
- 1/2 tablespoon lemon juice
- 1/2 tablespoon ground garam masala
- 1 tablespoon oil

Stuffing
- 8 tablespoons cooked Francelines puréed in a vegetable mill
- 1 tablespoon cashew nuts, chopped
- 1 tablespoon almonds, chopped
- 1 tablespoon raisins, chopped
- 1 tablespoon coriander, chopped
- salt
- 1/2 tablespoon red chilli powder
- 1 tablespoon ginger, chopped
- 1/2 tablespoon green chilli, chopped

Vineet is the first Indian to hold a Michelin star. He is a genuine potato fanatic and uses it in all his cooking.

1

Boil the Francelines in their skins in salted water. When they are cooked, drain and peel, then cut them in half and scoop out the centres with a melon baller. Fry them in the peanut oil.

2

For the marinade: blend all the ingredients together to a smooth mixture. Put the potatoes in and rub them well with the marinade. Leave to marinate for 4 hours.

3

For the stuffing: mix all the ingredients together and divide the mixture into 8 portions.

4

To finish: stuff the potatoes and cook them in a tandoor or oven for 8 minutes at 175°C.

'Serve with a green salad and lemon wedges.'

Wine suggestion: Riesling 1997, Cuvée Frédéric-Émile-Trimbach.

Potato Barbajuans

Bruno Cirino [La Turbie, France]

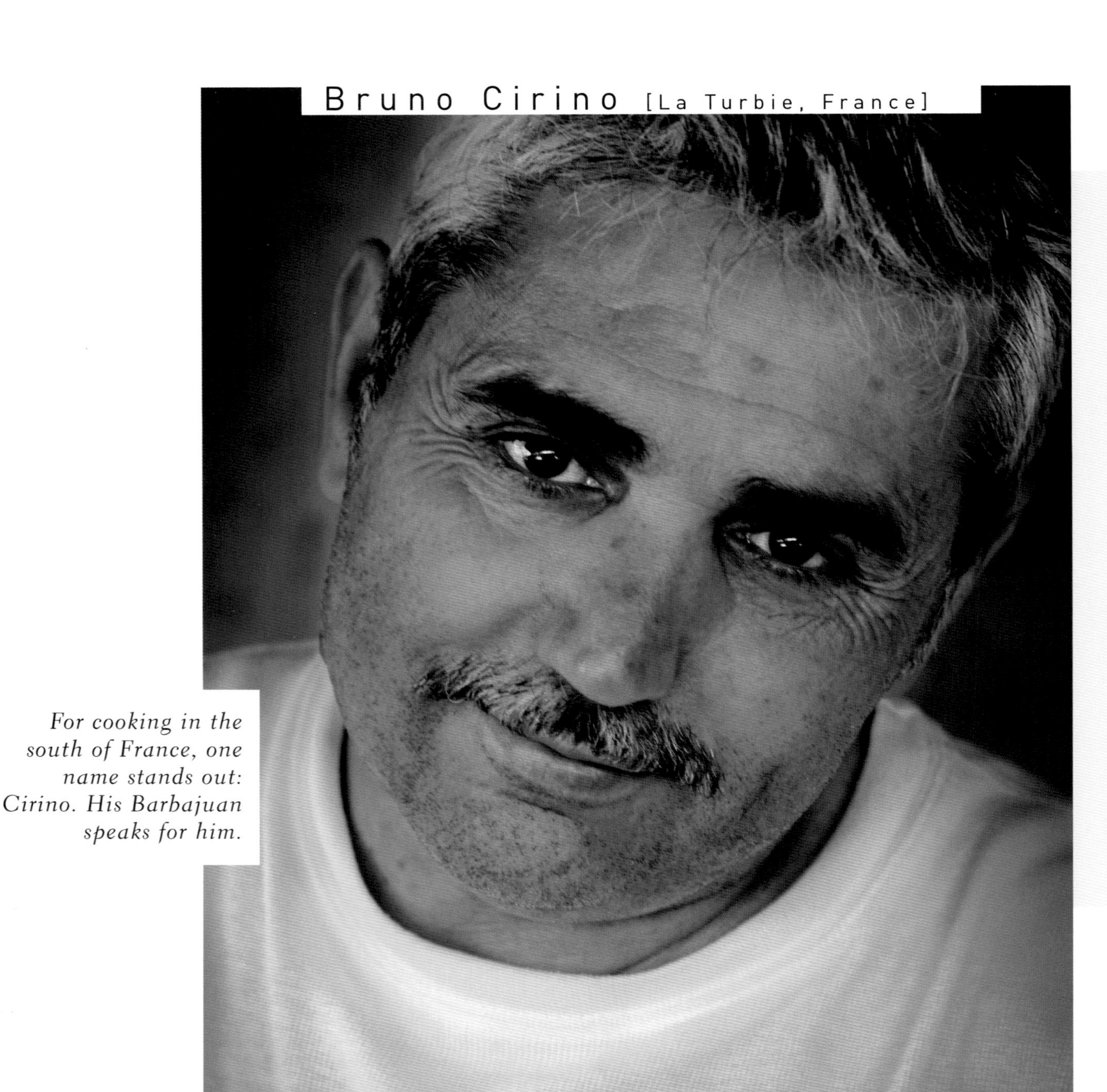

For cooking in the south of France, one name stands out: Cirino. His Barbajuan speaks for him.

Serves 4

Batter
- 250g flour
- 1 egg
- 60ml olive oil
- 60ml water
- 2g salt

Stuffing
- 400g Ratte potatoes
- 40g breadcrumbs (soft part only)
- 1/4 litre Ligurian olive oil
- 40g flat parsley, chopped
- 40g Parmesan, coarsely grated
- 60g fresh almonds blanched
- 50g black olives, pitted and blanched
- 5g thyme flowers, chopped
- 3 eggs
- 2 litres peanut oil for frying
- salt and pepper

1

For the batter: in a bowl, mix the flour, olive oil, egg and salt. Add the water a little at a time kneading the dough with the palm of the hand. When it is homogenous and fairly flexible, cover with clingfilm and leave to stand in the fridge for 3 hours.

2

For the stuffing: cook the unpeeled Ratte potatoes in lightly salted boiling water. Drain, and then peel very quickly (without letting them get cold). Arrange them side by side in a large, warmed dish, preferably terra-cotta. Sprinkle with the breadcrumbs. Saturate them with olive oil and mash with a fork. Add the parsley, Parmesan, roughly chopped almonds, the black olives and the thyme and eggs. Carefully mix and season with salt and pepper.

3

Roll out the dough to a thickness of 2mm. Cut into rectangles 8 x 4cm. In the middle of each rectangle, place a little sausage of stuffing, about 4cm long, using a forcing bag. Twist the rectangles of dough at either end to close them like sweets. Fry them on both sides in the oil for 2 minutes at 180°C. Drain, dry on kitchen roll and sprinkle with pepper. Serve warm as an appetizer.

Wine suggestion: Vin de Bellet, Clos Saint Vincent (R. Sicardi and J. Sergi).

Potato Bread

Éric Kayser [Paris, France]

This isn't bread: its cake!

Serves 4

- 2 egg whites, whipped
- 200g Charlotte potatoes
- 350g flour made up of 50% whole wheat, 50% strong white flour
- 150g rye flour
- 150g liquid leaven
- 10g fresh yeast
- 300ml water at 20°C

1

Boil the Charlottes in lightly salted water. When they are just cooked, peel and purée them very finely. Put in a bowl and set aside.

2

Put the 10g fresh yeast in a bowl. Dissolve it in 100g water at 20°C. Leave to stand at room temperature for 20 minutes or until fermentation starts.

3

Put the different types of flour in a bowl with the salt and mix well. Make a well in the centre and pour in the yeast mixture and the remaining water. Add the potato purée, the two beaten egg whites and mix the ingredients thoroughly.

4

Put the dough on a well-floured work service and knead for 10 to 12 minutes until it is firm. Put the dough back in a bowl, cover with a damp cloth and leave to stand at room temperature for 60 minutes.

5

Put the dough back on the well-floured work surface and shape it to resemble a short French stick. Place it on greaseproof paper on a baking tray. Lightly flour the top of the bread through a sieve. With the handle of a fork, make a few holes along it at regular intervals. Cover the bread with a damp cloth and leave to stand at room temperature for 2 hours.

6

Preheat the oven to 240°C. When it reaches the right temperature, put the bread in the oven and throw a little water into the oven (this is to help a crispy golden crust to form). Leave to cook for 35 to 40 minutes.

'Potatoes give this distinctive bread a soft, thick texture. Delicious spread with salted butter as an accompaniment to country cured meats or marinated fish.'

Wine suggestion: Patrimonio 2000, Domaine Leccia.

Caviar Potatoes with Sour Cream

Serves 4

- 8 small Charlotte potatoes, weighing about 30g each
- 20g imperial caviar

Stuffing
- 50g pickerel or chicken breast
- 70g single cream
- salt and pepper

Sour cream with chives
- 100g sour cream (1 measure of wine vinegar or lemon juice to 2 measures crème fraîche)
- 50g crème fraîche
- 1 tablespoonful chives, minced
- salt and Cayenne pepper
- juice of half a lemon
- 4 chive stalks

Hans Haas [Munich, Germany]

'To eat is a necessity. To eat intelligently is an art,' (La Rochefoucauld). Hans' cooking will initiate you into this art.

1

For the stuffing: chop all the ingredients in a blender and set aside.

2

Boil the Charlotte potatoes in their skins and leave to cool. Peel and cut them into two, then scoop out the centres using a melon baller. Stuff both halves of the potato with caviar and coat the sides with stuffing.

3

Put the two halves of the potatoes together. Roll them in the topping.

4

Brown the potatoes for a few seconds in olive oil. It is very important to make sure the potatoes are hot and that the caviar stays cold.

5

Arrange on a bed of sour cream with chives, and garnish with a few chive stalks.

Wine suggestion: Jurançon sec 2001, Domaine Cauhapé.

Spicy 'Papa Amarilla' Purée, Tuna, Avocado with a Sauce of Red Onions and Chilli Peppers

Ursula Makhlouf-Galidie [Lima, Peru]

Serves 8

Spicy 'papa amarilla' purée
- 1kg Amarilla (Mona Lisa) potatoes
- 90ml lime juice
- 125g chilli pepper (or 2 tablespoons Espelette pepper paste)
- 3 tablespoons olive oil
- salt and white pepper

Red onion and chilli pepper sauce
- 200g red onions
- 1 chilli pepper (or slice of Espelette pepper)
- 100ml lemon juice
- 2 tablespoons olive oil
- salt and black pepper

Light mayonnaise
- 1 whole egg
- 100ml peanut oil
- 1 teaspoon American mustard
- 2 teaspoons lime juice
- salt and black pepper

Stuffing
- 250g tuna bellies in olive oil
- 30g white onions
- 20g celery
- 125g lime mayonnaise
- salt and black pepper
- 2 avocados

Garnish
- 16 black Kalamata olives
- 2 hard-boiled eggs

Ursula has three passions: Lima, Paris and cooking. Here she presents a 100% New World dish that's not to be missed.

1

For the spicy 'papa amarilla' purée: wash, dry and cook the Amarilla potatoes in their skins in a saucepan of salted water and leave to simmer until cooked. Drain and peel, then purée in a vegetable mill (fine setting). Mix the potato purée with the lime juice, the chilli pepper paste and the olive oil. Season with salt and white pepper. Cover with clingfilm and put in the fridge for 30 minutes or until the purée is cool.

2

For the red onion and chilli pepper sauce: slice the red onion and chilli pepper finely. Soak the onion in a bowl of salted water for 30 minutes. Rinse and drain. Put the onion and pepper in a bowl and add the lemon juice and olive oil. Season with salt and black pepper. Put to chill in the fridge.

3

For the mayonnaise: put the whole egg, mustard and lime juice in a blender bowl and blend adding a drizzle of olive oil. Season with salt and pepper, blend and put in the fridge.

4

For the stuffing: dice the onion and celery quite small. Mix them in a bowl with the tuna and a few drops of lime and mayonnaise. Season with salt and black pepper.

5

To arrange: divide the purée into two on a piece of clingfilm and cover each half with it. Roll out both halves to a thickness of 1cm making them rectangular. In a rectangular dish, lay a base of purée after removing the clingfilm, and cover it with the stuffing. Lay thin slices of the avocado on top and lightly spread with mayonnaise. Cover with the second rectangle of purée. Arrange black olives and discs of hard-boiled eggs along the top as well as the onion and chilli pepper sauce. Serve cold.

'You can replace the tuna with crab meat, prawn or steamed vegetables.'

Wine suggestion: Pouilly Fumé Blanc, 2001 Chaillons (Didier Dagueneau).

New Potatoes with Eggs, Parmesan Gratin and Truffles

Luisa Valazza [Soriso, Italy]

Serves 4

- 4 medium-sized Charlotte potatoes
- 5 egg yolks
- 80g truffles
- grated Parmesan
- milk
- salt
- pepper

Why, until this year, were Italy's only two 3-star chefs women? Come and taste Luisa's dishes and you will find out why she is one of them. NB: this recipe was originally designed to use white truffles; alas, we arrived too late in the season and were deprived of the 'tartufi d'Alba'.

1

Boil the Charlottes in their skins in lightly salted water for 30 minutes. Peel and set aside.

2

With a spoon, make a hole in the potatoes the size of an egg yolk. (Keep the centres.) Set aside the hollowed-out potatoes in a warm place.

3

Purée the potato centres in a vegetable mill, add the milk, a spoonful of grated Parmesan and an egg yolk. The purée should be light.

4

Place an egg yolk in the hollow of the cooked potatoes, and then stuff with the potato purée. Put the potatoes in a dish and brown for 5 minutes.

5

Take out the potatoes, arrange them on a plate and grate the truffles over them.

Wine suggestion: Piemontese Barolo Marasco 1997 (Franco Martinetti).

Crisp Paupiette of Sea Bass in a Barolo Sauce

Daniel Boulud [New York, US]

If restaurants are improving in New York nowadays, it's all thanks to chefs like Daniel, who have banned the word IMPOSSIBLE from their vocabulary.

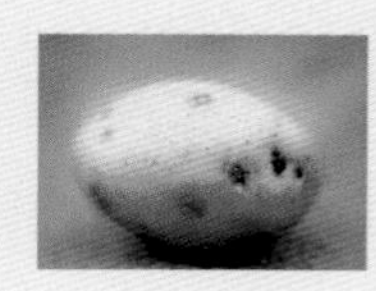

Serves 4

Sauce
- bones of 4 sea bass
- 1 teaspoon oil
- 115g shallots, peeled and chopped
- 115g button mushrooms, cut (heads only)
- 1/2 sprig fresh thyme
- 250ml chicken stock
- 750ml Barolo or other red wine
- 1 teaspoon double cream
- 115g unsalted butter
- 1 pinch sugar
- 1 teaspoon chopped chives

- 4 sea bass fillets, weighing 200g each, with the skin removed
- 1 sprig thyme, chopped
- 2 large BF15 potatoes, peeled
- 50g butter

- 2 teaspoons butter
- 2 leeks (white part only), finely chopped

- salt and pepper
- 2 sprigs thyme

1

For the sauce: heat the oil in a casserole dish over a high heat. Add the sea bass bones, roast them for 4-5 minutes over a high heat, then add the shallots, mushrooms and thyme and leave to cook again for 4-5 minutes stirring frequently. Mix in the chicken stock and reduce till dry. Add the red wine, bring to the boil and leave to reduce gently to half. Sieve the juices in a conical sieve and reduce until there are 2 tablespoonfuls left. Set aside.

2

For the BF15 potatoes: cut the potatoes into rectangles (without washing them, the starch will help them bind together). Cut each rectangle into fine slices using a mandolin (you should get 16 slices per potato - you need eight to wrap a sea bass fillet). Mix the potato slices with 1 spoonful of melted butter and salt. Place a 25-cm square of greaseproof paper on the work surface. Choose 8 slices of potato of the same size and overlap them to form a rectangle.

3

Cut the sea bass fillets into rectangles (13 x 5cm). Season with salt, pepper and 2 spoonfuls of chopped thyme. Place a fish fillet in the middle of a potato rectangle and fold the sides of the rectangle over the fish, wrapping it completely. Repeat for all the other fillets.

4

Put the butter in a frying pan over a medium heat, mix in the leeks and sweat them for about 4 minutes until they are tender. Season with salt and pepper. Keep them warm.

5

Preheat the oven to 220°C. Melt the remaining two spoonfuls of butter in a non-stick frying pan over a high heat. Add the sea bass paupiettes and sauté until they turn golden-brown (about 3-5 minutes for each side). If the fish is very thick, finish cooking them in the oven for 4-5 minutes.

6

Meanwhile, add the cream to the sauce, stir and bring to the boil over a low heat. Then whisk in the butter, sugar, salt and pepper. Strain through a conical sieve with a fine mesh and keep them on the heat.

7

Arrange the leeks in the middle of the plate and drizzle the sauce around them (about 2 teaspoonfuls). Place the sea bass paupiettes on the leeks and decorate with half a sprig of thyme. Sprinkle the plate with chopped chives.

Wine suggestion: Pinot Noir, Flowers Keefer Ranch 2000, Sonoma Coast.

Potato Gnocchi with Sweet Pepper Preserve and Sea Urchins

Carlo Cracco [Milan, Italy]

Carlo can turn his hand to novelty but also to classics like these gnocchi.

1

For the peppers: peel the peppers and cut them into 12 strips. Arrange on a dish and sprinkle with extra-virgin olive oil. Roast in the oven at 75°C for 45 minutes.

2

Boil the Bintje potatoes in a saucepan of lightly salted water. Peel the potatoes and purée them through a vegetable mill. Mix the purée with the flour, eggs, nutmeg, salt and grated Parmesan. Stir the mixture as little as possible (to avoid making it hard and sticky).

3

Divide the purée in two and keep it warm. Shape it into logs 1.5cm in diameter and cut smaller, 2-cm logs from them. Roll them between the palm of your hands. Then plunge the gnocchis into a saucepan of salted boiling water and leave to cook for 3 minutes or until they rise to the surface, then fish them out using a slotted ladle, refresh in ice-cold water and arrange them on a dish.

4

Brown the gnocchis in a lightly buttered, non-stick frying pan.

5

Sauté the spinach with a little olive oil. Tip the spinach into a dish and arrange the gnocchis over them and the strips of pepper, the veal and the sea urchins.

Wine suggestion: Chardonnay Rarita 1991, Cantina di Terlano.

Serves 4

- 500g Bintje potatoes
- 150g flour
- 20g Parmesan
- 2 eggs
- 15g fine salt
- 1 pinch nutmeg
- 40g spinach
- 4 sea urchins
- 2 peppers
- 16 pieces steamed veal

Potatoes and Free-Range Chicken with Preserved Lemons and Black Cumin

It was bound to happen: by dint of gathering old Moroccan recipes from a buried culinary heritage, Fatema has become their keeper, and she is more than happy to let you in.

Fatema Hal [Paris, France]

Serves 4

- 1kg free-range chicken cut in four pieces
- 1kg Ratte potatoes
- 3 good teaspoons cumin
- 2 onions
- 2 tomatoes
- 1 large preserved lemon
- 7 tablespoons olive oil
- 1.5 teaspoons salt
- 1.5 pinches pepper
- 1.5 pinches ginger
- 1 bunch coriander
- 3 glasses water
- 1 pinch saffron strands

1

Wash, drain and chop the coriander. Slice the onions finely. Crush half the cumin and leave the other half for later.

2

Rub the chicken pieces with the crushed cumin and put them in a cooking pot. Add the olive oil, ginger, salt and pepper and brown the chicken pieces over a high heat, turning every 5 minutes.

3

Add the three glasses water and the saffron strands. Bring to the boil. Add the chopped coriander, the remaining whole cumin seeds and wedges of the preserved lemon. Put the lid on the pot and leave to simmer over a low heat for 20 minutes.

4

Peel the Ratte potatoes, wash them and cut them lengthwise into 4. Wash the tomatoes, remove the skins and dice.

5

Add the potatoes and tomatoes to the pot, cover and leave to cook for 20 minutes over a low heat.

6

Arrange the chicken pieces in a dish, pile the potatoes on top to form a dome and pour the sauce over them. Make sure the cumin seeds and lemon wedges are fully visible in the dome. Serve hot.

Wine suggestion: Red Riad-Jamil from the Meknès cellars.

Ravioli of Red Imola Potatoes, potato sauce and culatello di zibello

Valentino Marcattillii [Imola, Italy]

Valentino has a heart of gold, a keen sensitivity to the lands he visits every morning and genuine affection for anyone he has trained, as Michael White of the Osteria Fiamma in New York is the first to point out.

Serves 4

- 400g ravioli dough
- 100g pancetta, finely cut
- 500g Franceline potatoes, steamed
- 1/2 bay leaf
- 2 tablespoons extra-virgin olive oil
- 100g grated Parmesan
- 1 egg
- salt
- pepper
- nutmeg
- 100g culatello di zibello (Italian cured meat) cut into very fine strips
- 200ml chicken stock

1

Brown the pancetta with the bay. Add 400g of the steamed Franceline potatoes and brown over a gentle heat for 10 to 15 minutes. Season and leave to cool. Then add the grated Parmesan, nutmeg and egg and mix everything together.

2

Roll out the ravioli dough thinly. Arrange little piles of stuffing on half the strip of dough, fold over the other half and close up the ravioli cushions, then cut them out with a fluted pastry cutter. Cook in salted boiling water. Drain and set aside.

3

Blend the remaining 100g Franceline potatoes with the chicken stock, add the extra-virgin olive oil and season.

4

Place the ravioli in a dish, pour the chicken sauce over them and add the thin strips of culatello di zibello, a little grated Parmesan and a drizzle of olive oil.

Wine suggestion: Sangiovese di Romagna 2001.

Yamanoimo in Caviar Parcels

Serves 4

- 15g Yamanoimo (Mona Lisa) potatoes
- 15g Nagaimo (sweet potato)
- 2 eggs
- 80g flour
- 250ml milk
- 2g salt

- 10g Roseval potatoes, puréed
- 5g Roseval potatoes, diced
- 5 salmon eggs
- 10g caviar
- 1 spoonful chopped chives
- 10g sour cream
- 20g crème fraîche

- 15 salmon eggs
- one caper branch
- a few slivers of red radish
- a few cornichons, finely sliced
- a few spring onion bulbs, finely sliced
- a few slivers anchovy
- a little chopped shallot
- curly parsley
- yolk of 1 hard-boiled egg, chopped
- white of 1 hard-boiled egg, chopped
- avocado oil

The most French of Japanese chefs pays tribute to French haute cuisine.

1

Grate the Yamanoimo and Nagaimo potatoes finely, then add them to the mixture of salt, eggs, flour and milk. Strain through a conical sieve to obtain a smoothish batter. Cook a pancake in a non-stick frying pan with a drop of peanut oil.

2

Spread the 10g Roseval potato purée over the pancake. Lay the caviar, 5 salmon eggs, 5 cubes of Roseval potatoes and chopped chives on top of the purée.

Kiyomi Mikuni [Tokyo, Japan]

3

Close up the pancake with a boiled chive stalk and brown it slightly.

4

Put the pancake in the centre of the plate, then, working from the pancake outwards, arrange circles of chopped shallot, chopped egg yolk, chopped egg white and finally, chopped parsley. Decorate the rest of the plate with the other garnishes (caper branch, red radish, cornichon, onion and anchovy).

5

Sprinkle the remaining 15 salmon eggs over the pancake and add a drizzle of avocado oil.

Wine suggestion: Riesling 1999, Domaine Zind-Humbrecht.

Chicken Potato with Five Flavours

The smell of the 'five flavours' wafts over the 'Mer de Chine'. Seak Chan Wong has brought this recipe from the world's number one potato producer. We've had rice, now for the potatoes.

Seak Chan Wong [Paris, France]

Serves 4

- 2 Bintje potatoes
- 2 chicken thighs
- 2 tablespoons potato flour
- salt and pepper

Sauce
- 1/2 teaspoon glutamate
- 1/2 teaspoon sugar
- 1/2 teaspoon black soy sauce
- 1 cube chicken stock
- 1/2 teaspoon ground Sichuan spice

- 2 tablespoons sunflower oil
- 1 clove chopped garlic

- coriander

1

Blanch the Bintje potatoes for 8 minutes in salted water, drain, then peel and dice them. Fry them for 5 minutes and set aside.

2

De-bone the chicken thighs and cut them into fine pieces. Season with salt and pepper. Roll them into little balls with the potato flour.

3

For the sauce: mix the ingredients in a bowl and set aside.

4

Heat a wok or high-sided frying pan, add the oil and chopped garlic and brown until they acquire a fine golden colour. Add the diced potato, chicken balls and the sauce. Sauté over a high heat for about 1 minute.

5

Pile them into a plate and scatter sprigs of coriander over them.

'You can make this dish without glutamate.'

Wine suggestion: Anjou 2001, Les Bergères (Jo Pithon).

Chatouillard Potatoes

Benoît Guichard [Paris, France]

Serves 4

- 12 Agria potatoes
- peanut oil for frying
- fine sea salt
- fleur de sel

Our thanks to Benoît for bringing us one of Escoffier's recipes that was never photographed.

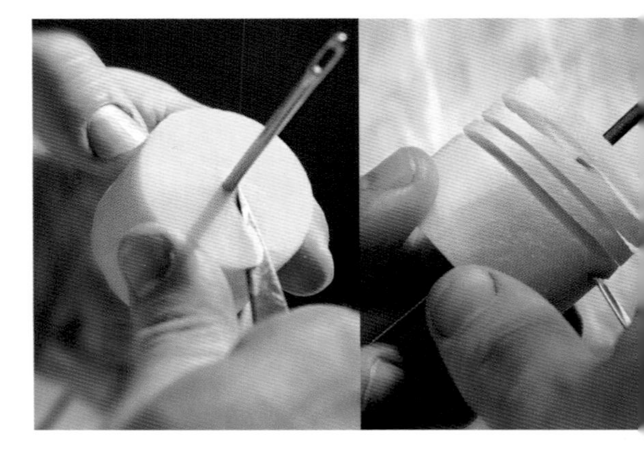

The basic technique

1

Peel the Agria potatoes and cut them into fat cylinder shapes, then spear them through the centre with a darning needle. Cut the potatoes into spirals starting from the top; move the point of the knife in a circular movement around the needle to create long, even spirals of rings 3mm thick. Then wash the spirals and leave to dry.

2

Poach the spirals in the frying oil at 140°C for 12 minutes, then plunge them straight into another pan of very hot oil until they puff up and turn golden brown. Drain on a cloth and season with a mixture of fine sea salt and fleur de sel.

Sand Roses

Michel Troisgros [Roanne, France]

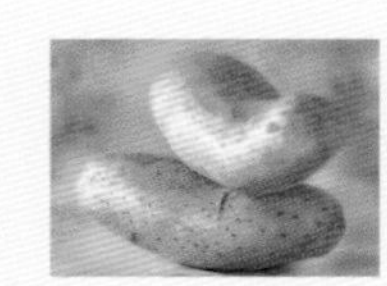

Serves 6

- **3 large Mona Lisa potatoes, weighing 300g each**
- **250g butter**
- **fine salt**

1

Peel the Mona Lisa potatoes and leave to stand in cold water. Trim the ends and cut them in half. With a knife, form short fat logs from the potatoes about 5cm in diameter and 5cm long.

2

Cut around the log with a sharp knife working to make a long thin ribbon. Be careful not to break it. Then roll up the ribbon into a coil. Set aside in cold water. Make six pieces.

3

For the clarified butter: cut the butter into chunks and put it in a bain-marie. When the butter melts, remove impurities that come to the surface and the whey (whitish) at the bottom. Strain.

4

Drain the coils on a clean cloth. Delicately open out the coils to form a rose shape. Dip the roses one at time in the butter to coat them all over. Arrange them side by side in an oven-proof frying pan or non-stick dish. Roast them in the oven at 220°C for 15 minutes, basting them frequently during cooking with the hot butter. The part in contact with the pan will turn golden and crispy; the upper part will remain soft.

5

Carefully remove the roses with a spatula, drain and salt them while still hot.

This recipe has been on the menu at Troisgros for over thirty years, and like their Salmon with Sorrel, belongs to the heritage of French cooking in the same way as Escoffier's Chatouillard Potatoes.

Soufflé Potatoes with Cinnamon Sugar

Jean Brouilly [Tarare, France]

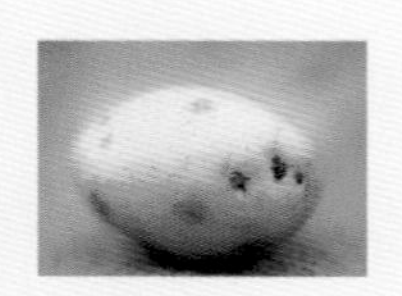

Serves 4

- 2 BF15
- 200g icing sugar
- 10g ground cinnamon
- peanut oil for frying

166 years after it was first invented, on the occasion of the opening of the railway from Paris to Saint-Germain-en-Laye, Jean and his head confectioner, Pascal Goutaudier, take a fresh look at souffléd potatoes. A real autumnal and original treat that goes well with caramel, cinnamon or gingerbread ice cream.

1

Make the BF15s oval in shape then cut them into very regular, 3mm thick slices and dry them on a cloth to get rid of any moisture. Set aside.

2

Prepare the cinnamon icing sugar by mixing the two ingredients together. Set aside.

3

Heat two pans of oil, one to 120°C the other to 160°C. Plunge the potatoes two at a time into the 120°C oil stirring with a circular motion to froth up the oil. Then plunge them into the 160°C oil, stirring in the same way until the potatoes puff up. Lay them on kitchen towel without overlapping.

4

Sprinkle the souffléd potatoes with the cinnamon icing sugar.

Wine suggestion: Muscat de Rivesaltes.

Purée of Ratte Potatoes, Welsh Onion Flowers and Frogs Legs with Herb Parmentier

Roland et Alexandre Gauthier [Montreuil-sur-Mer, France]

Roland (on the right) cooks to his heart's content now that his son, Alexandre, has come to join him. He made this Parmentier especially for us, and his cooking had never been so expressive and his interpretation of the regional specialities so inspired.

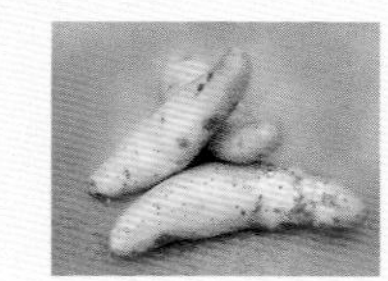

Serves 8

Purée
- 10 Rattes potatoes
- 200g lightly salted butter
- 20 spring onion flowers
- salt and pepper

Parmentier
- 1 leek
- 3 Ratte potatoes
- 1litre chicken stock
- 1 clove smoked garlic
- 1 tablespoon olive oil

Green herb sauce
- 1/4 bunch flat parsley
- 4 lovage leaves
- 4 chive stalks
- 2 branches fresh coriander
- 4 leaves salad burnet
- 8 sorrel leaves
- 200ml chicken stock
- 100ml extra-virgin olive oil

- 16 frogs' legs
- 200g flour
- 4 egg yolks
- 200g breadcrumbs
- 10g salted preserved lemons
- 100ml single cream
- grapeseed oil for frying

1

For the purée: wash and peel the Ratte potatoes, put them in a saucepan of cold salted water and bring to the boil. Drain and mash with a fork. Fry the butter until it turns light brown. Season and set aside.

2

For the Parmentier: wash and chop the leek and potatoes. Sweat the leek then add the potatoes. Soften them in the chicken stock and leave to cook with the whole garlic clove. When they are cooked, take out the garlic clove and blend the Parmentier. Set aside.

3

For the green herb sauce: blend the flat parsley, lovage, chives, coriander and salad burnet with the chicken stock, then add the sorrel. Add the extra-virgin olive oil at the end to intensify the green colour and bring out the flavours.

4

Make drumsticks from the frogs' legs and push in a tiny cube of preserved lemon. Bread them in the flour, egg yolks and breadcrumbs. Fry in the grapeseed oil.

5

To finish: heat the Parmentier. Meanwhile, place on a plate a portion of the reheated purée and decorate with the spring onion flowers, then arrange the frogs' leg fritters. Add some of the sauce to the Parmentier. Just before putting the Parmentier on the plate, emulsify with a spoonful of whisked single cream.

Wine suggestion: Prieuré-Saint-Jean-de Bébian, unfiltered, 1998 (B. Lecouty).

Tapas of Charlotte Potatoes and Black Truffle in a Jar

Alberto Herraîz [Paris, France]

The province of La Mancha has given the world two famous men: the first, Cervantes, went off to write in a prison cell in Seville; the other, Alberto Herraîz, came to Paris to work in his restaurant as a chef. Truffles and potatoes were good enough for Olivier de Serres, and we enjoyed them too.

1

Clean and wash the Charlotte potatoes and black truffles. Using a circular pastry cutter, cut discs of potato and black truffle of different thicknesses but the right size to fit the jar. Fill the jar with alternating layers of potato and black truffle discs. (Put the thickest discs in the bottom and end up with the thinnest, finishing with potato.)

2

Cut the rest of the black truffle into small cubes and arrange them on the last disc in the jar. In a bowl, blend the red wine vinegar, olive oil, fleur de sel and the pepper. Pour this mixture into the jar and close.

3

Cook in a bain-marie for 2 hours or steam oven for 70 minutes.

4

Open the jar, spear the potato and truffle discs with a skewer and remove from the jar. Arrange the skewer on a plate, serve hot and sprinkle with the cooking juice.

'This recipe is an example of how we see tapas: as a dish in its own right with its own flavours and accents.'

Wine suggestion: Viña Tondania Blanco, Gran Reserva, 1981, Rioja.

Serves 4

- 4 black truffles, weighing 40g each
- 4 Kennebec (Charlotte), 40g each
- 40ml red Cabernet-Sauvignon vinegar
- fleur de sel
- pepper
- olive oil

Chinese Potatoes

Michel adapted his famous Chinese Tomatoes to give us Chinese Potatoes. It was a sure bet! A must as a starter.

Michel Troisgros [Roanne, France]

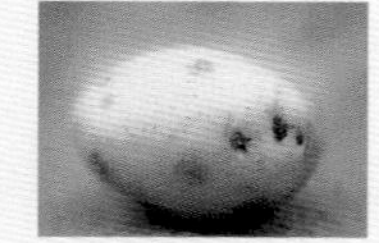

Serves 4

- 2 large BF15 potatoes
- 2 litres peanut oil for frying
- 150g sugar
- 1 teaspoon white sesame seeds
- 1 lime
- 10g fresh ginger

Batter (prepare a few hours in advance):

- 100g flour
- 100g cornflour
- 150ml beer
- 100ml water
- 15g baking powder
- 1 egg yolk
- 1 pinch salt

'You should get another pair of hands to help you make the sauce.'

1

For the batter: in a large bowl, whisk in one after the other the flour, cornflour, baking powder dissolved in beer, the water and the egg yolk. Sieve the mixture to get rid of the lumps. Cover the bowl with clingfilm and chill it in the fridge for a few hours. Just before serving, give it another whisk.

2

Cut the ginger into thin sticks.

3

Peel the BF15 potatoes and cut them into matchsticks making them as regular as possible. You should make 20 sticks. Roll the sticks one at a time in the batter. Plunge 10 of them into the deep-fryer (preheated to 160°C). When they turn crispy, drain on kitchen towel. Repeat the operation for the remaining 10.

4

Heat the sugar in a frying pan to obtain a pale caramel. Add a drizzle of olive oil, then plunge the chips into it. Sprinkle the potato sticks with sesame seeds and shake the pan with a circular movement to make sure they are completely coated. Remove the sticks one by one with tweezers and put them straight into a large bowl of iced water for a few seconds. Then arrange them on a plate. Sprinkle with lime zest and ginger.

'These little mouthfuls of caramel are delicious as a starter. The soft potato complements the crunchy caramel.'

Wine suggestion: Bourgogne Aligoté, Domaine Aubert-et-Paméla-de-Villaine.

Focaccia of Vitelotte and Rosemary

Serves 4

- 200g Vitelotte potatoes (boiled for garnish)
- 40g Vitelotte potatoes (raw)
- 450g flour
- 80ml milk
- 240ml water
- 100ml extra-virgin olive oil
- 35g beer yeast
- 20g salt
- 5g rosemary

Carlo Cracco [Milan, Italy]

Together with Joan Roca in Gijón, Jacques Decoret in Vichy, Pascal Barbot in Paris and Heston Blumenthal in Bray, Carlo Cracco is one of the musketeers of European nouvelle cuisine.

1

Grate the raw potatoes and mix with the flour, milk, water, olive oil, beer yeast, salt and rosemary to make the dough. Knead the dough for 6 minutes. Leave to stand.

2

Form balls of dough and place small cubes of the boiled potatoes on top. Leave the dough to rise on a baking tray greased with olive oil.

3

Bake in the oven at 180°C for 12 minutes.

Wine suggestion: Chardonnay Rarita 1991, Cantina de Terlano.

Salad of Ratte Potatoes with Herbs and Garden Flowers in a Sorrel Cream

Where does Jean get all these ideas?
Riding up the Beaujolais hills!

1

Cook the potatoes in their skins in salted water.

2

For the mustard dressing: mix 1 egg yolk and the mustard and lemon juice, then add the olive oil, salt and pepper. Set aside in the fridge.

3

Peel the potatoes and mash with a fork. Season with mustard dressing, chopped herbs and minced flowers.

4

For the sorrel cream: boil an egg for 3 minutes, wash the sorrel and chop coarsely. Put everything into the blender with a very little water and salt and pepper, then blend with the grape seed oil.

5

Pour the sorrel cream onto the plate, then pile a small dome of potatoes in the middle. Decorate with herbs and flowers.

'To make this more substantial, you can make a base of fried potato spirals'.

Wine suggestion: White Beaujolais, 2002, Château des Ganges.

Serves 6

- 1kg Violay (Ratte) potatoes
- 2 eggs
- 1 tablespoon coarse-
  grained mustard
- 100ml olive oil
- 100ml grapeseed oil
- 20g fresh sorrel
- salt
- pepper
- edible flowers (pansies, nasturtiums, • garlic or chive flowers)
- herbs
- 1 lemon

Salad of Bleue de la Manche, Sorrel Snails and Camembert Cream

Serves 4

- 4 small Bleue de la Manche (Vitelotte) potatoes
- 1 onion
- 1 bouquet garni
- coarse salt
- 100ml single cream
- 100g Camembert
- 50g nettles or sorrel
- 20 cooked snails
- 4 bunches savory or dill
- 100g mixed lettuce
- fine salt and milled pepper

Vinaigrette
- 2 tablespoons hazelnut oil
- 1 tablespoon cider vinegar
- salt and pepper

Michel Bruneau [Caen, France]

1

Wash and boil the Bleue de la Manche potatoes in their skins with the bouquet garni, the onion and the coarse salt.

2

Peel them, then cut them in half lengthwise and scoop out the centres with a melon baller so that you can stuff them. In a saucepan, heat the cream with the Camembert crust, then pour through a conical sieve. Add in small cubes of the middle of the Camembert, leave to melt and blend with a whisk adding the nettles and snails.

3

Stuff the potatoes with 5 snails per person, pour a little of the Camembert cream over them and put in the oven for 5 minutes. Fry the savory bunches in the peanut oil and set aside.

4

Arrange the potato on a bed of salad seasoned with the vinaigrette, pour a little cream over it and lay the fried savory on top.

Wine suggestion: Les Arpents du Soleil, Vin de Normandie (M. Samson).

For Michel, this extraordinary recipe is the ultimate regional speciality. Snails + potatoes + Camembert make a tasty combination that could only come from Normandy.

Gilles Choukroun [Paris, France]

Serves 4

- 4 Charlotte potatoes
- 6 Ratte du Touquet potatoes
- 4 Vitolette potatoes
- 2 Lady Chrystal potatoes
- 2 Francine potatoes
- 2 Charlotte potatoes

- 2 sheets filo pastry
- 100g butter
- 1 tablespoon white sesame seeds
- 500ml oil for frying
- 2 tablespoons olive oil
- 1 tablespoon minced chives
- 250ml milk
- 50g curly parsley
- cumin powder
- chilli powder
- fleur de sel
- milled Pendjab pepper

Gilles is one of those hosts who will see that you don't overdo it but he has also decided that life is too short to make do with miserable fare.

1

For the Charlotte potatoes: make a purée by mixing the cooked potatoes with half its weight in butter. Season with salt.

2

For the Ratte potatoes: steam 4 potatoes in their skins, then cut them into 5mm slices. Cook the remaining two in the salted water, then peel and mash them with a fork. Mix them with the white sesame seeds and spread this mix over two sheets of buttered filo pastry. Cut into triangles and cook in the oven for 5 minutes.

3

For the Vitolette potatoes: finely dice 2 raw potatoes and mix with the olive oil, chives and a pinch of chilli powder. Thinly slice the 2 remaining potatoes and fry the slices.

4

For the Lady Chrystal potatoes: make a milkshake. Steam the potatoes, then blend with the milk and parsley. Season with salt, pepper and a pinch of cumin.

5

For the Francine potatoes: cut them into thin sticks and fry them to make chips.

6

For the Charlotte potatoes: finely slice them lengthwise, then, using a paper doily as your guide, make little holes and fry them to make chips.

7

To finish: pour the milkshake into 4 small glasses. Serve the rest of the potatoes as you like.

Wine suggestions: Blanc Fumé de Pouilly 2000, Cuvée Silex (Didier Dagueneau).

Salad of Vitelotte Potatoes, Breton Lobster and Mousse of Ratte Potatoes

1

For the salad: finely dice the vegetables and mix them with a little olive oil, salt and pepper. Cook the asparagus and set aside.

2

Boil the Vitelottes in their skins in salted water. When they are cooked, peel them and cut in half. Season with coarse salt and set aside on a plate covered with clingfilm stretched tight.

3

Cook the lobsters in a court-bouillon for about 10 minutes, then shell them and cut them into chunks.

4

For the mousse of Ratte potatoes: boil the potatoes in their skins in salted water. Blend everything and pour through a fine-mesh conical sieve. Taste the jus and mix with the egg white and single cream. Put everything into a soda siphon.

5

For the potato biscuits: peel the Bintje potatoes and cut them into very fine crisps using a mandolin. Brown them in the clarified butter and put them in the oven to dry out at 65°C until they are crispy. Season with salt.

Alex, Arnold's son, represents the fifth generation of chefs in the Hanbuckers family. One for the record: his father forbade him to study at a hotel and catering college.

Alex Hanbuckers [Bruges, Belgium]

Serves 4

- 2 tomatoes
- 8 pitted olives
- 25g capers
- 2 green onions
- olive oil
- 1 bunch green asparagus
- 6 Vitelotte potatoes
- coarse salt for coating
- 4 Breton lobsters, weighing 1.5kg each

Mousse
- 250g Ratte potatoes
- 100g egg white
- 150g single cream

Potato biscuits
- 1 large Bintje potato
- clarified butter

Turmeric butter
- 20g root turmeric
- 200ml chicken juices
- 100g Mascarpone
- fresh herbs: chervil, chives, lemon balm, tarragon
- salt and pepper

Balsamic syrup
- 200g balsamic vinegar
- 60ml concentrated apple juice
- 1 shot red wine vinegar

6

For the turmeric butter: chop and cook the turmeric in the chicken juices. Blend, sieve it and reduce by three quarters. Mix the Mascarpone with the chopped fresh herbs. Work it into the turmeric sauce to obtain a 'butter'. Garnish the potato biscuits with this butter.

7

For the balsamic syrup: reduce the balsamic vinegar, concentrated apple juice and red wine to obtain a syrup.

8

To finish: start by placing a tablespoonful of the salad on a plate, followed by half a Vitelotte potato, two asparagus tips, then the lobster and finally the potato mousse. Repeat the operation twice more for each plate to create three separate domes. Decorate with a chive stalk and a drizzle of balsamic syrup. For added colour and texture you can top each dome with a small quenelle of fish roe.

Wine suggestion: Panizzi 1998, Vernaccia di San Giminiano.

Vitelotte Potato Rissoles, Marinated Tuna Bellies, Garlic Cream with Watercress Salad

Serves 4

- 300g Vitelotte potatoes
- 200g tuna bellies
- 400g coarse white salt
- 150g fresh bread (with the crusts removed)
- 2 eggs
- peanut oil for frying
- 1 bunch watercress
- 100ml peanut oil
- 100g spring garlic
- 50ml extra-virgin olive oil
- 100ml single cream

Marinade
(prepare 24 hours in advance):
- 100g yuzu juice
- 5g thinly sliced ginger
- 10ml nuoc-mâm (fish sauce)
- 20ml soy sauce
- 25ml olive oil
- 20ml sesame oil
- 1 pinch garlic powder
- salt and Sarawak pepper

Patrice Hardy's rissoles are exquisite. That's all there is to say!

Patrice Hardy [Paris, France]

1

Put the Vitelotte potatoes to bake in the oven in the coarse salt for about 40 minutes at 200°C. When they are cooked, dry them and purée them in a vegetable mill. Adjust the texture and season.

2

For the marinade: mix the ingredients in a bowl as though for a vinaigrette.

3

Dice the tuna bellies to cubes 12mm thick, season and leave to marinate for 10 minutes in the marinade.

4

Sponge off the pieces of tuna then coat them in the purée making little balls about 3cm in diameter. Chill in the refrigerator.

5

Sort the cress keeping the small leaves for the salad and blanching the rest. Chill and blend to a coulis with the peanut oil. Season.

6

Peel the garlic and cook it in the single cream, season and blend with the olive oil. Sieve the mixture and set aside.

7

Heat the deep-fryer to 180°C. Roll the potato balls in the beaten egg then in the breadcrumbs and plunge them in the hot oil for 3 minutes. Drain and serve.

Wine suggestion: Chablis 1993, Domaine Picq (old vines).

Iced Soup of White Vegetables

Hirohisa Koyama [Tokyo, Japan]

Serves 4

Potato cream
- 500g Bintje potatoes
- 1/2 onion
- 5 small turnips
- 100g white radishes
- 50g celery stalk
- 5 white asparagus

Broad bean cream
- 500g broad beans
- 1/2 onion
- 5 small turnips
- 100g white radishes
- 50g celery stalk
- 5 white asparagus
- salt, pepper

The maestro of kaiseki *cuisine (Japanese haute cuisine) was keen to grace our book with his venerable gastronomic presence. We were duly honoured.*

1

For the potato cream: wash and peel the Bintje potatoes and other vegetables then cut them into pieces. Put them in a casserole dish with water and simmer. Take the vegetables out of the soup, blend the vegetables and pour through a sieve. Pour the soup into the vegetable purée and whisk until it is creamy, without adding any fats. Leave to cool.

2

For the broad bean cream: proceed as for the potato cream.

3

Divide a bowl down the middle using a piece of cardboard wrapped in aluminium foil. Pour the potato cream into one side and the broad bean cream into the other. Carefully remove the board.

Drink suggestion: Saké Kinpu.

Turbot Chunks, Potato Purée with Black Truffles, Country Herbs and Monkfish Tripes

A highly original recipe with unusual flavours and accents by the most Japanese of young Italian cooks.

Serves 4

1 turbot, weighing 4kg

Court-bouillon
- 5litres water
- 50g salt
- 50g carrots
- 50g onions
- 50g celery

Tripe
- 200g monkfish tripe
- 2g lardons
- 1 tablespoon sage
- 1 tablespoon lemon thyme
- 1 tablespoon celery, diced small
- 1 tablespoon wild fennel, chopped
- 1 tablespoon parsley, chopped
- 1 tablespoon onion, chopped
- 1 tablespoon carrot, diced small
- 10ml olive oil
- 10g smoked fish
- 10g grated Parmesan
- salt and pepper

Country herbs
- 150g white beetroot
- 50g endive
- 30g Ratte potatoes
- 20ml olive oil
- 5g garlic
- salt and pepper

Purée
- 300g Charlotte potatoes
- 30g butter
- 50ml milk
- 10g black truffles
- salt and pepper

1

Remove the head and tale from the turbot, then lift the skin from both sides. Cut it into 4 regular 300g chunks, then, using a pair of scissors, remove the first vertebra from either end of each chunk.

2

For the court-bouillon: cook all the ingredients for 15 minutes in a saucepan.

3

Tripe: clean the monkfish tripe and soften them in the hot court-bouillon for 15 minutes then leave to cool and cut them into very thin strips. Put the tripe in a bowl and mix with the lardons, sage, lemon thyme, diced celery, wild fennel, parsley, onion, carrot and olive oil. Brown over a low heat in a saucepan. Stir in the smoked fish, season and add the grated Parmesan. Cook until the sauce thickens.

4

Country herbs: wash and cut the beetroot and endive into sticks 2cm wide. Boil them in salted water. Peel and chop the Ratte potatoes, and cook them al dente in salted water. When they are cooked, put the 20g olive oil and the garlic in a frying pan, add in the potatoes, beetroot and endive, and brown.

5

For the purée: cook the 300g Charlotte potatoes in salted water, drain and peel. Purée them in a vegetable mill, then stir in the butter and milk, season and add the chopped black truffles.

6

Season the turbot cutlets with salt and olive oil and cook in the oven at 200°C until they reach 50°C in the middle. Put the potato purée either side of a non-stick frying pan and brown the turbot in the centre.

7

Arrange the turbot cutlets on the purée and country herbs, add 2 spoonfuls of tripe and serve.

Wine suggestion: Verdicchio dei Castelli di Jesi Classico Superiore, DOC, Gaiospino 2001, Saffolo (Lucio Canestrari).

Moreno Cedroni [Marzocca-di-Senigallia, Italy]

Risotto-style Parmentier with Fresh Morels in a Jus of Roast Veal

1

For the jus of veal: chop the veal trimmings into pieces weighing 50g each brown them in the olive oil and butter until they turn pale gold (make sure not to burn the butter). Take off the grease by removing the cooking butter. Put the shallots and garlic cloves in a high-sided frying pan, sweat them, then deglaze with the Port, reduce the liquid until nearly dry and add the chicken stock a little at a time. Reduce by three quarters, then strain through a muslin chinois and add the cooking butter. Simmer gently. Keep hot.

2

For the morels: clean the morels then plunge them in the boiling water for 15 seconds, refresh and drain. In a high-sided frying pan, sweat the shallots with 30g butter without browning. Add the morels and heat for about 30 seconds. When the morel juices have evaporated, add the fresh herbs, salt and pepper.

Michel del Burgo [Paris, France]

One risotto can hide another. With a flourish, intelligence and taste, Michel shares his passion for juggling with flavours.

3

For the Parmentier: heat 10g butter and a drizzle of olive oil in a high-sided frying pan, add the potato cubes and leave to sweat gently. Stir in the chicken stock and cook until the liquid evaporates. Finish the risotto by thickening it with the potato purée, Mascarpone and grated Parmesan (the consistency should be slightly runny). At the last minute, add the whipped cream and fine salt.

4

To serve: put the potato risotto on four plates, arrange the morels tastefully and sprinkle everything with the veal jus and a drizzle of olive oil.

Wine suggestion: Blanc 2000, Château d'Aupilhac.

Serves 4

- 400g Agria potatoes, cut into cubes 5 x 5mm
- 1/4 litre chicken stock infused with the morel stalks
- 1 tablespoon Mascarpone
- 1 tablespoon potato purée
- 1 tablespoon whipped cream
- 20g grated Parmesan
- 10g butter
- 1 drizzle olive oil

Veal jus
- 1kg veal trimmings
- 6 minced shallots
- 5 cloves garlic
- 1/2 litre Port
- 1 litre chicken stock
- 30ml olive oil
- 80g butter
- fine salt

Morels
- 600g washed morels, caps only
- 2 minced shallots
- 30g butter
- 1.5 tablespoons herbs (chervil, chives, parsley)

Yukon Gold Purse in a Black Truffle Skin

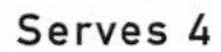

Serves 4

- 800g Yukon Gold (Charlotte) potatoes
- 2 egg whites, beaten to form peaks
- 12 prawns, peeled
- 250ml American sauce sprinkled with 1 tablespoon chopped tarragon
- 250ml chicken stock thickened with cornflour (1/2 tablespoon cornflour)
- 4 truffles, weighing about 20g each, finely sliced
- salt
- white Pendjab pepper
- grated nutmeg
- juice of half a lemon
- extra-virgin olive oil
- 4 bowls 12cm in diameter

Taïra Kurihara [Paris, France]

The Buster Keaton of Tataki invented this dish just for us. The photo matches the dish: elegant, discreet, refined and above all delectable.

1

Grate and salt the Yukon Gold potatoes, season with lemon juice and leave to drain through a sieve for 10 minutes.

2

Season the potatoes with the salt, pepper, a pinch of nutmeg and add the beaten egg whites. Stir well and set aside.

3

Cut the prawns into three, then put them in a non-stick frying pan with a few drops of olive oil to sear them. Deglaze with the American sauce.

4

Line a bowl with clingfilm, lay half the slices of truffle on it and cover with a layer of grated potato. Place 3 prawns on top cut in three. Cover with the other half of the truffle slices and potato. Close up the clingfilm, seal it tightly and knot the mouth. Repeat the operation for the other purses.

5

Steam the 4 purses in a couscoussier for 10 minutes over a medium heat. Serve immediately and drizzle the chicken stock around the purses.

'Don't forget to warm the plates.'

Wine suggestion: Savennières.

Parmentier of Calamares

Like Pascal Barbot in Paris or Heston Blumenthal in Bray, Joan is for us one of the leading nouvelle cuisine chefs... with Catalan accents. This new recipe is a perfect example.

Joan Roca [Gijón, Spain]

Serves 4

- 1 medium-sized squid
- 250g cuttlefish
- 750g Jaerla (Mona Lisa) potatoes
- 100ml olive oil
- 100ml single cream
- 2 onions
- 2 carrots
- 1 tomato
- 1 litre water
- 2 tablespoons olive oil
- 1 teaspoon chilli powder
- 100g butter

1

Clean the squid carefully and cut it into rings 0.5 cm thick. Set aside the tentacles for the sauce.

2

Season the squid rings with the chilli powder and wrap them tightly in clingfilm in a cylinder shape and put to chill in the refrigerator.

3

Boil the Jaerla potatoes in their skins in a saucepan of salted water for 30 minutes. Drain, peel and purée in a vegetable mill. Season with olive oil and add the single cream.

4

Wash and dice the vegetables. Put them in a saucepan with a little olive oil and brown them for a few minutes. Add the squid tentacles and the water and simmer for 30 minutes. Sieve the sauce and emulsify with the butter cut into small chunks.

5

Pile the purée into the middle of a shallow soup bowl, cut fine discs of squid and lay them on the purée to form a circular mosaic. Brown under the grill or in the salamander for a few minutes.

6

Meanwhile, sauté the cuttlefish in a frying pan with a drizzle of olive oil.

7

Before serving, place the cuttlefish around the purée and surround with the sauce.

Wine suggestion: Corullon Mencía 2000, El Bierzo (J. Palacios).

Russian Banana Fingerling, New York Red Bliss and Désirée Potatoes with a Kumomoto Oyster Emulsion and Iranian Osetra Caviar

1

Cook the Yukon Gold potatoes in their skins in salted water for 30 minutes. Drain, peel and purée them in a vegetable mill. Season with olive oil, salt, pepper and a few drops of lemon juice then add the crème fraîche.

2

Place the Russian Banana Fingerling potatoes on a sheet of aluminium foil and add the thyme, olive oil, salt and white pepper and wrap them up. Bake in the oven for 40 minutes at 220°C. When they are cooked, cut them into fine slices.

3

Finely grate the fennel bulb, season with olive oil, lemon, salt, pepper and fennel seeds.

4

Sauté the chives in olive oil and leave to cool. Blend the chives and add 20g cold olive oil. Season with salt and pepper.

5

Boil the Désirée potatoes in their skins in salted water for 30 minutes. Drain, peel and purée in the vegetable mill. Mix with the oysters, their juices and the vegetable stock. Add the milk and season with salt, white pepper and fennel seeds. Add the 60g butter and heat everything at 75°C. Season with the lemon juice. Emulsify before serving.

There's no stopping Charlie 'Globe-trotter's' taste for transcultural flavours, as this half-Asian, half-American dish shows.

Charlie Trotter [Chicago, US]

Serves 4

- 120g Iranian Oestra caviar

Yukon Gold purée
- 100g Yukon Gold (Charlotte) potatoes
- 50g crème fraîche
- a few drops lemon juice

Russian Banana Fingerling potatoes
- 4 Russian Banana Fingerling (Ratte) potatoes
- thyme

Fennel purée
- 80g fennel bulb
- 1 pinch fennel seeds
- 2 tablespoons olive oil
- juice of half a lemon

Chive purée
- 1 bunch chives
- 20ml olive oil

Désirée potatoes and oyster emulsion
- 4 medium-sized Désirée (Franceline) potatoes
- 10 small oysters
- 1/2 litre milk
- 1/2 litre vegetable stock
- 60g butter
- juice of half a lemon
- 10 fennel seeds

Roasted New York Red Bliss potatoes
- 2 New York Red Bliss (Roseval) potatoes
- 1 shot of white vinegar
- 1 pinch chopped parsley
- 3 tablespoons olive oil

- 14g chive shoots
- 28ml extra-virgin olive oil
- olive oil
- salt and white pepper

6

Cut the New York Red Bliss potatoes into thin slices 3mm thick. Sauté them in the olive oil until they turn golden brown, then season with the white vinegar, chopped parsley and salt. Leave to cool at room temperature before serving.

7

Present as in the photo.

Wine suggestion: Blanc de Blanc Brut NV (Jacques Selosse).

Slowly Cooked Cod, Potato Noodles with Crème Fraîche, Vodka and Caviar

Serves 4

- 600g cod fillets
- 6 large Yukon Gold (Charlotte) potatoes
- 500ml crème fraîche
- 60ml lemon juice
- 125ml vodka
- 1 branch rosemary
- 4 tablespoons caviar
- salt and Cayenne pepper
- olive oil
- fleur de sel

1

Peel the Yukon Gold potatoes and cut them into noodles using a mandolin. Wash them in cold water then blanch in salted boiling water for 10 seconds (they should still be crunchy) and refresh in ice-cold water. Set aside.

2

Season the fish fillets, put them in an oven-proof pan with a knob of butter and put them to cook through in the oven at 200°C.

3

Heat the crème fraîche with the rosemary, a pinch of salt, the lemon juice and the vodka, then whisk lightly.

4

Season the noodles with salt, Cayenne pepper, lemon juice and olive oil and gently heat them through. Take the fish fillets out of the oven and sprinkle with a pinch of salt.

5

In a small bowl, arrange the noodles and place the fish fillets on top. Pour a spoonful of sauce around the noodles and add a tablespoon of caviar to the fillets.

Wine suggestion: Grüner Veltliner Federspiel Hinter Der Burg 2000, Präger.

Jean-Georges Vongerichten [New York, US]

Jean-Georges is the archetypal modern chef: 'with it' and absorbing every influence wherever he goes. In a word, he is aware. 'Made in Alsace', this star chef cooked this souvenir from his holidays in Mongolia before our very eyes.

Big Chips, Hint of Hay

Serves 4

- 600g Bintje potatoes
- 320g hay soaked over night in water
- peanut oil for frying

When we started this book, we decided that recipes for purée or chips would be a blind alley it was best not to take. Heston proved us wrong! Hats off to Mr Blumenthal.

1

Drain the soaked hay on a tea towel. Put the dry hay in a stainless steel dish and flambé it with a torch until it gives off a smoky smell.

Heston Blumenthal
[Bray-on-Thames, England]

2

Put the hay in a saucepan and add enough water to cover it by 4cm. Bring to the boil and simmer over a low heat for 15 minutes. Take the saucepan off the heat and leave to infuse for 20 minutes.

3

During this time, cut the Bintje potatoes into chips 1.5cm thick and rinse them in running water for 5 minutes. Add the cubes to the hay and cook over a low heat until they are cooked (on the point of disintegrating). Take out the potatoes carefully and place them in a drying machine to get rid of the excess water (if you do not have one, put them on a non-stick baking tray and leave to cool in the air).

4

Heat the peanut oil to 140°C in a deep fryer or high-sided frying pan, add the potatoes and cook until a dry crust forms but do not let them brown. Remove the potatoes and put them on kitchen towel for a few seconds before returning them to the drying machine (or leaving them to cool on a baking tray).

5

Increase the temperature of the oil in the deep fryer to 190°C and plunge the potatoes back in until they are crispy and golden. Put them on a plate covered in kitchen towel, season with salt and serve.

'This process can seem a bit long, but it produces great results. Chips lose their crunchiness because of the steam escaping from the centre. This makes the crust softer. I attempted several methods to try and reduce the level of humidity in the centre of the chips. You can cut the potatoes into regular cubes or, as in the photo, into big chips. You don't get the same aesthetic effect but you do get a wider range of flavours.'

A drying machine

Sweetened Potato Purée with Vanilla

Ferràn Adrià [Roses, Spain]

MA-GIC (pronounced 'ma-hic') is a word that sums up both the chef and his cooking. This recipe may make you want to venture into the world of Catalonian cooking around Roses.

Serves 4

Potato purée
- 200g Charlotte potatoes
- 130g butter at room temperature
- 50g single cream (35% fat)
- 40g caster sugar
- 1 vanilla pod
- coarse sea salt

Emulsified yolk
- 1 egg yolk
- 1 pinch caster sugar
- 12ml hot water

To decorate:
- 4 vanilla pods

'Guests should smell the vanilla as they eat this dessert.'

1

Peel the Charlotte potatoes, cut into wedges and place in a saucepan of cold water. Cook over a medium heat for 20 minutes.

2

Drain the potatoes and purée through the fine setting of a vegetable mill. Put the purée into a saucepan, add the single cream and butter at room temperature and cook over a low heat stirring well.

3

Split the vanilla pod lengthwise down the middle and scrape the seeds out of the pod. Add the vanilla seeds and sugar to the purée and stir thoroughly.

4

Whisk the egg yolk in a bowl over hot water (a bain-marie) until it turns white. Add the sugar and continue whisking. Add the hot water a little at a time while the mixture emulsifies.

5

To serve, place a soup spoonful of potato purée in a shallow bowl, sprinkle with a pinch of coarse sea salt, drizzle the emulsified egg yolk around the purée and place a vanilla pod at the edge of the plate.

Wine suggestion: Champagne Gosset, Chardonnay Pinot Noir, Grande Réserve, AOC Champagne AŸ.

Purée of Francine Potatoes, Caramel, Green Tea Ice Cream

Pascal Barbot [Paris, France]

When Pascal turns his kitchen into a research laboratory, the results are always positive.

Serves 4

- 300g Francine potatoes
- salt
- sugar

Caramel sauce
- 100g sugar
- 15g lightly salted butter
- 50g single cream
- 40ml cooking water from the potatoes

Green tea ice cream
- 1/2 litre whole milk
- 6 egg yolks
- 120g sugar
- 1 teaspoon top-quality green tea powder

1

Boil the Francine potatoes in their skins for 25 minutes in salted and sugared water. Peel and purée in a vegetable mill while still hot (perform these operations at the last minute).

2

For the caramel sauce: melt 100g sugar in a saucepan to obtain a pale gold caramel and add the 15g butter, single cream and water from the potatoes. Boil for 1 minute and set aside.

3

For the green tea ice cream: bring the milk to the boil and set aside. Beat the egg yolks with the sugar until they turn white. Pour the hot milk over the egg-sugar mix and cook at 84°C in a bain-marie. Add the green tea and put it in an ice-cream maker.

4

Serve the potato purée on a plate while still warm together with the caramel sauce and green tea ice cream.

Wine suggestion: Vouvray Demi-Sec 1996, Domaine Uhuet-L-Mont (Noël Pinguet).

Quinoa Cones with Syrup of Roots and Potato Mousse

1

Quinoa cones: line the inside of 8 metal cones with greaseproof paper. Make the Italian meringue. When it is cold, mix in the muesli. Fill the cones with this mixture making sure not to press everything together. Dry them in the oven for 30 minutes at 100°C. Carefully turn out. Leave to cool and delicately set aside.

2

Potato jam: wash the Franceline potatoes and boil them with their skins for about 25 minutes. Prepare a syrup with sugar, water, pectin and cinnamon. Bring to the boil and skim. Split the vanilla pod in two, scrape out the seeds with a knife and add to the syrup. As soon as the potatoes are cooked, drain, peel and purée in the vegetable mill. Add them to the syrup and bring to the boil for 5 minutes. Pour into a jar and close the lid.

3

Potato mousse: bring the concentrated milk and butter to the boil. Remove from the heat and add the gelatine, which has first been softened in cold water, and 250g of potato jam. Leave to cool. When the mixture has solidified slightly, work in the whipped single cream. Put to chill in the refrigerator.

4

Sweet onion preserve: prepare a syrup by boiling the water and sugar. Peel and wash the onion. Cut it into fine slices 6mm thick. Blanch the onion slices in salted boiling water. Drain and put them in the boiling syrup. Store over night in the refrigerator. Next day, drain the onion slices and reduce the syrup by boiling it for 10 minutes. Pour the syrup over the onion slices and again store over night in the refrigerator. Repeat the operation one last time next day. Drain the onion slices and remove the excess syrup with your fingers. Lay them on a sheet of greaseproof paper and put them to dry over night at 60°C. Store in a tin in a dry place.

5

Sweetcorn sauce: blend the ingredients hard and boil for 10 minutes. Blend again then sieve and put in the refrigerator.

6

Beetroot juice: boil all the ingredients together. Sieve the spices and reduce to a syrupy consistency. Set aside.

7

At the last minute, warm the sweetcorn sauce and froth up using a hand-held blender. Cover the base of a plate with the beetroot juice and sweetcorn sauce. Stand a quinoa cone in it. In a terrine, whisk the potato mousse to a smooth consistency. Using a 12mm piping bag, trail a thread of potato mousse around the cone as in the photo. Create a second cone of potato mousse. Finish with the slices of preserved onion and a few sweetcorn kernels that have first been blanched for 2 minutes.

Wine suggestion: Vin de Paille d'Arbois 1995 (Jacques Puffeney).

Michel Bras [Laguiole, France]

A sophisticated dessert inspired by the New World and a treat for the Old Continent.

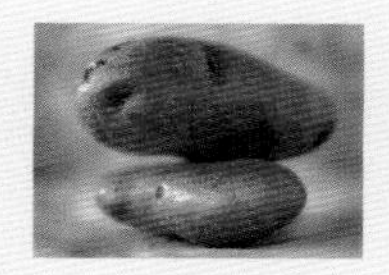

Serves 4 people

Quinoa cones
- 150g Italian meringue
- 350g cruncho (muesli)
- 150g puffed quinoa

Potato jam
- 500g Franceline potatoes
- 400g caster sugar
- 100ml water
- 8g pectin
- 1 pinch cinnamon powder
- 1 vanilla pod
- salt

Potato mousse
- 250g potato jam
- 200g unsweetened concentrated milk
- 70g melted butter
- 15g gelatine leaves
- 400g single cream

Sweet onion preserve (prepare 4 days beforehand):
- 30g sugar
- 300ml water
- 1 Lézignan onion (large white variety)
- salt

Sweetcorn sauce
- 200ml milk
- 40g sweetcorn
- 40ml grapeseed oil
- 20g sugar

Beetroot juice
- 50ml vinegar
- 100ml beetroot juice (from 200g centrifuged beetroot)
- 20ml oil
- juice of half and zest of an orange
- 100g caster sugar
- 3g coriander
- 1 juniper berry
- 1 broken clove
- 1 pinch pepper
- salt
- 1 star anis
- a few sweetcorn kernels

Recipe published with the kind permission of Editions du Rouergue.

Potato Dynamite Stick, Parsley Ice Cream and Passion Fruit Juice

1

Parsley ice cream: blanch the flat leaf parsley, then refresh and drain. Mix the egg yolks, sugar and glucose and whisk everything. Stir in the hot milk and cook 'à la nappe' (very slowly to allow the custard to thicken). Add the single cream and blanched parsley. Blend and sieve the cream and put it in an ice-cream maker.

2

Passion fruit juice: cut open the fruits, take out the seeds and sieve the juice. Reduce the juice to half with the icing sugar. Put in the refrigerator.

3

Potato mousse: cook the Belle de Fontenay, potato flakes, milk and cream until half cooked. Blend and add the remaining milk and the sugar and cook again for 5 minutes. Stir in a pinch of grated nutmeg and the gelatine (first soaked in cold water). Sieve the sauce, then pour it into a soda siphon and put in the fridge.

Jacques Decoret [Vichy, France]

Watch out, this man is dynamite! Jacques has by turns blown up, centrifuged, dehydrated and souffléed his potatoes. You have been warned!

Serves 8

Parsley ice cream
- 350ml milk
- 80g single cream
- 4 egg yolks
- 50g sugar
- 10g glucose
- 80g flat leaf parsley

Passion fruit juice
- 80g passion fruit
- 6g icing sugar

Potato mousse
- 100g Belle de Fontenay potatoes
- 20g potato flakes
- 310ml milk
- 60g icing sugar
- 110g single cream
- 2 leaves gelatine
- 1 pinch ground nutmeg

Potato sugar
- 95g potato flakes
- 110g fondant
- 40g caster sugar
- 4g cream of tartar
- 20g glucose

Potato jam
- 4 large BF15
- sugar syrup (500ml water to 300g sugar)

4

Potato sugar: mix the fondant, caster sugar, glucose and cream of tartar in a saucepan and cook to obtain a pale caramel. Stir in the potato flakes and leave to cool. Put the cooked sugar in the blender to obtain a powder. Make a rectangular stencil. On a sheet of non-stick or greaseproof paper, sieve the powder through the stencil spreading it evenly with a pastry brush. Cook in the oven at 190°C until the powder melts and turns colourless. Then roll it over a greased stainless steel tube to make tube-shaped.

5

Potato jam: cut the BF15 lengthwise into slices 4mm thick. With a 4cm pastry cutter, cut out 48 discs. Make strands by cutting 8 potato sticks 5cm wide. Put them into the sugar syrup to crystallise. When they are crystallised, take out the potato discs, drain and caramelise them gently in a non-stick frying pan.

6

Arrange 6 caramelised potato discs in each plate. Garnish the potato sugar tube with the mousse, add the strand and lay them on the discs. Drench with passion fruit juice and decorate with a scoop of parsley ice cream.

Wine suggestion: Condrieu 1999, Domaine A.-Perret.

Potato Croquettes with Araguani Chocolate Sauce and Red Pepper Jam

Hervé Galidie [Paris, France]

Hervé came up with this dessert especially for the book before (we sincerely hope!) adding it to the menu of his restaurant. Potato, chocolate and pepper: Peru on a plate!

Serves 4

Ganache
- 150g araguani chocolate
- 150g single cream

Charlotte potato paste
- 325g Charlotte potatoes
- 1 egg
- 30g caster sugar
- 50g flour

Coating
- 2 eggs
- 10g flour
- 110g chopped almonds
- 1/2 litre peanut oil for frying

Pepper jam
- 100g red peppers
- 50g honey
- 1 lime

Salad
- 1 bunch fresh mint
- 1 bunch fresh parsley
- 16 acacia flowers
- 1 lime
- olive oil

1

Ganache: grind the chocolate very finely. Bring the single cream to the boil and pour it over the ground chocolate. Mix well. Set aside at room temperature and leave to thicken. Cover a plate with clingfilm, fill a piping bag with the ganache and make 6cm x 1.5cm tubes, then put them in the fridge.

2

Charlotte paste: peel the Charlottes, cut them into quarters, then put them in a saucepan of cold water and leave to cook. When they are cooked, put them on a tray to dry and put them in the oven for 15 minutes at 180°C. When they are dry and still hot, purée them in a vegetable mill and stir in the egg, flour and sugar. Mix everything to obtain a paste of an even consistency.

3

Potato croquettes: divide the paste into four and roll out each section on a floured work surface (to prevent the paste sticking). Cut out rectangles 7.5cm wide, 6cm long and 3mm thick. Lay 1 chocolate stick on one of the rectangles and roll up completely. Repeat the operation 7 times. Put on a tray covered with clingfilm and place them in the refrigerator to chill for 30 minutes.

4

Roll the croquettes in the flour then in the beaten egg and finally in the crushed almonds, then put them in the refrigerator for 30 minutes. Fry the croquettes in the peanut oil at 160°C for 3 or 4 minutes or until they turn a fine golden colour.

5

Meanwhile, cut the peppers into four, peel them and remove the seeds. Blend the pepper quarters in a centrifuge juicer. Reduce the pepper juice with the honey to obtain a jam. Stir in the lime juice.

6

Place 2 croquettes on a plate, add a spoonful of jam on the side of the plate and decorate with a few mint and parsley leaves. Season with olive oil and lime juice. Add 4 acacia flowers and serve.

Wine suggestion: Rivesaltes Rouge 1999 Vintage, Domaine Pujol.

Iced Soup of Charlotte Potatoes, Corn and Lemon

So much media attention hasn't spoiled Pierre's culinary and creative flair one bit. Here is the proof.

Pierre Hermé [Paris, France]

1

Charlotte potatoes cooked in saffron juice: peel the Charlotte potatoes and dice them to make 4mm cubes. Boil them for 10 minutes then drain. In a saucepan, boil all the other ingredients and cook with the potatoes for 8 minutes until they are tender but firm and not collapsed. Leave over night in the refrigerator to chill and macerate.

2

Slices of poached lemon: make a syrup by boiling the water and sugar. Cut the ends off the lemons and using a very sharp knife or a small slicer, slice them very thinly. Put them in a gratin dish and pour over the boiling syrup. Cover with clingfilm and leave to macerate over night. Next day, drain before using.

3

Cooked Charlotte potatoes: in a pressure cooker, cook the potatoes in the 500ml water for 8 minutes. Peel them and lay them in a gratin dish. Cook in the oven at 180°C for 5 minutes.

4

Charlotte potato and lemon ice cream: in a saucepan, make a syrup by boiling the water, sugar and lemon zest. Strain. Mash the cooked potatoes in a vegetable mill. Put the potato purée in a saucepan and whisk in the milk. Pour in the hot syrup and lemon juice. When it is completely cold, put everything into an ice-cream maker and store in the freezer.

Serves 8

Charlottes cooked in saffron juices
(prepare a day in advance)
- 750g Charlotte potatoes
- 500ml mineral water
- 50g caster sugar
- 50ml grapefruit juice
- 50ml lemon juice
- 12 saffron strands
- zest of one slice of orange
- 4 grinds white Pendjab pepper

Slices of poached lemon
(prepare a day in advance):
- 300g lemons
- 150g caster sugar
- 300ml water

Cooked Charlotte potatoes
- 500g Charlotte potatoes
- 500ml water

Charlotte and lemon ice cream
- 150g cooked Charlotte potatoes
- 200g caster sugar
- 200ml water
- zest of one lemon
- 200ml lemon juice
- 250ml milk
- 50g butter

Iced lemon soup
Part I
- 300g drained semi-preserved lemons
- 50ml lemon juice
- 100ml orange juice
- 100ml water
- 70g caster sugar
- 6 grinds white Pendjab pepper
- 8 drops chilli sauce

Part II
- 200g cooked Charlotte potatoes
- 240g single cream
- 40g butter

Vitelotte potato crisps
- 3 Vitelotte (purple) potatoes
- icing sugar

To finish
- 200g drained tinned sweetcorn
- 25g salted popcorn
- 12 crushed violet sweets
- fresh mint

5

Iced lemon soup: blend all the ingredients in Part I as finely as possible. Part II: mash the Charlotte potatoes in a vegetable mill then whisk in the cream then the butter cut into small pieces. Make a smooth purée. Blend to obtain a very smooth soup then strain through a medium sieve. Leave to cool.

6

Vitelotte potato crisps: preheat the oven to 100°C. Slice the Vitelotte potatoes very finely. Lay a sheet of greaseproof paper on a baking tray and sprinkle with icing sugar. Arrange the potato slices on it and sprinkle with icing sugar. Bake in the oven for 30 minutes. Turn them over and cook for another 30 minutes.

7

To finish: scatter the sweetcorn and diced Charlottes cooked in saffron juice into a shallow soup bowl; pour the iced lemon soup over them. Sprinkle with popcorn, minced mint and crushed violet sweets and place a large sausage of Charlotte potato and lemon ice cream in the bowl. Decorate with Vitelotte crisps.

Wine suggestion: Muscat Corse or Muscat Beaume-de-Venise.

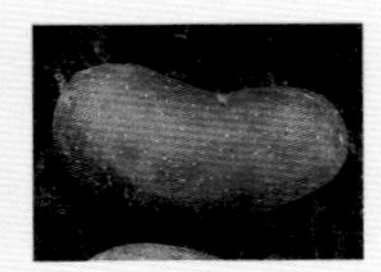

Patathivier

Serves 4

Lemon-almond cream
- 1 egg
- 40g sugar
- juice of one lemon
- 50g butter
- grated zest of half a lemon
- 80g ground almonds

To bind
- 25g beaten egg
- 5ml milk
- 4g cornflour

Potatoes
- 250g Roseval
- 1 litre water
- 50g melted butter
- 2 teaspoons caster sugar

1

Lemon-almond cream: put the egg and sugar in a bowl and whisk immediately for about 3 minutes until the mixture turns white. In a small heavy-bottomed pan, bring the lemon juice to the boil on a moderate heat. Pour the boiling lemon juice over the white egg-sugar mixture and whisk, then pour everything back into the pan. Gradually bring to the boil stirring gently all the time with a spatula. As soon as it boils, count 5 seconds, then pour the mixture into the blender. Add the butter and lemon zest and blend for 30 seconds. Put the lemon cream aside in a bowl then stir in the ground almonds.

2

Line a soup bowl with clingfilm and pipe the lemon-almond cream over it using a piping bag. Ideally, you should obtain a disc 10 to 12cm in diameter and 1 to 2cm thick. Cover with clingfilm and put the cream in the freezer for 1 to 2 hours for the cream to harden.

3

To bind: meanwhile, whisk the egg, milk and cornflour in a bowl, then sieve. Set aside.

4

Potatoes: brush the Rosevals with their skins on under running water. Slice them very thinly with a mandolin to obtain regular, translucid slices less than 1mm thick. Put the slices straight into a bowl of cold water. Bring 1litre water to the boil over a high heat. Drain and plunge the potato slices into boiling water. When they come back to the boil, count 5 seconds then remove from the heat. Leave the potatoes to cool in their cooking water; they will be cooked but still firm and flexible.

5

When the potatoes are cold, drain them through a sieve, then spread them on a cloth to get rid of the moisture. To make it easier to arrange the tart, it is best to start by making three or four piles of potato slices according to size: big, medium, little and tiny. Divide each pile into two so that you can make two identical rose patterns of potato.

6

From a sheet of aluminium foil, cut out a disc of a diameter 4cm greater than your mould of lemon-almond cream (e.g., the disc would be 14cm for a mould 10cm in diameter). Grease this disc thoroughly and scatter a teaspoonful of caster sugar over it. Arrange the potato in concentric circles so that they each overlap by a third to form a rose shape. The small slices go in the centre, the bigger ones around the edge. Start by laying a slice of potato in the centre of the circle. This will be your guide, which you will then follow to create the first circle (about 6 to 8 slices) working clockwise. Make a second concentric circle in the same way (about 12 to 16, i.e., twice the number you used before), working anti-clockwise. Repeat the operation to make concentric circles right out to the edge of the foil disc (3 or 4 circles depending on how big a potato you used).

7

To finish: turn out the disc of hardened lemon-almond cream and brush it all over with egg. Brush the rose of potatoes on its upper side, too. Centre the cream disc on the rose-shape and lay another potato rose over it to cover it completely and make the Patathivier. Coat the Patathivier liberally with melted butter and sprinkle a teaspoon of sugar over it, then put it to chill in the refrigerator for at least an hour and for a maximum of 24 hours.

8

To cook: Preheat the oven to 220°C, put the baking tray in the middle of the oven. Put a non-stick flan mould in the freezer for a few minutes, then coat it with a brushing of melted butter (the mould will help the Patathivier stick together). Remove the Patahivier from the fridge and turn it over in the flan mould with the aluminium foil now on top. Put on the centre of the baking tray. Cook for 1 or 2 minutes, then carefully peel off the aluminium foil and roast for 40 to 50 minutes. Sprinkle with icing sugar and wait until the Patathivier is cool before turning it out.

'The great thing about this recipe is that it harmonises a very noticeable flavour of roast potatoes - that distinctive taste of rather well done crisps - with the sweet accents of the cream.'

Wine suggestion: Caprice d'Antan, Guillac (R. Plageolle).

Previously known for his 'world cooking', Paul should now be recognised for his 'surprise cooking'. His Patathivier has some good surprises in store for you.

Paul Pairet [Paris, France]

Potato Notebook

The Chefs and their Addresses

Ferràn Adrià, page 172
El Bulli
Cala Montjoi, 17480 Roses (Spain) – tel: (34) 972 15 04 57;
email: bulli@elbulli.com; website: www.elbulli.com

Pascal Barbot, page 174
L'Astrance
4, rue Beethoven, 75016 Paris – tel: 01 40 50 84 40

Christophe Beaufront, page 84
L'Avant-Goût
26, rue Bobillot, 75013 Paris – tel: 01 53 80 24 00

Bénédict Beaugé, page 86
website: bbeauge@miam-miam.com

Vineet Bhatia, page 108
Zaika
1 Kensington High Street, London W8 5SF
tel: 0 20 779 56 533; email: info@zaika-restaurant.co.uk;
website: www.zaika-restaurant.co.uk

Heston Blumenthal, page 170
The Fat Duck
High Street, Bray-on-Thames SL6 2AQ
tel: 01628 580333; website: www.fatduck.co.uk

Daniel Boulud, page 120
Daniel
60 East 65th Street, New York, NY 10021 (United States) –
tel: 1 (212) 288 0033; website: www.danielnyc.com

Michel Bras and Mémé Bras, pages 100 and 176
Route de l'Aubrac, 12210 Laguiole – tel: 05 65 51 18 20;
email: michel.bras@wanadoo.fr; website: www.michel-bras.com

Jean Brouilly, pages 136 and 146
Restaurant Jean Brouilly
3 *ter*, rue de Paris, 69170 Tarare – tel: 04 74 63 24 56;
email: restaurant.jean-brouilly@wanadoo.fr;
website: www.tarare.com/brouilly

Michel Bruneau, page 148

Michel del Burgo, page 160

Yves Camdeborde, page 80
La Régalade
49, avenue Jean-Moulin, 75014 Paris – tel: 01 45 45 68 58

Raquel Carena, page 88
Le Baratin
3, rue Jouye-Rouve, 75020 Paris – tel: 01 43 49 39 70

Moreno Cedroni, page 158
La Madonnina del Pescatore
11, Lungomare-Italia, 60017 Marzocca-di-Senigallia (Italy) –
tel: (39) 071 69 82 67; email: madonninadelpescatore@tin.it

Gilles Choukroun, page 150
Café des délices
87, rue Assas, 75006 Paris – tel: 01 43 54 70 00

Bruno Cirino, page 110
Hostellerie Jérôme
20, rue Comte-de-Cessole, 06320 La Turbie –
tel: 04 92 41 51 51

Carlo Cracco, pages 122 and 144
Cracco-Peck
4, via Victor-Hugo, 20123 Milan (Italy) –
tel: 02 87 67 74; email: cracco-peck@peck.it;
website: www.peck.it

Jacques Decoret, page 178
Jacques Decoret
7, avenue Gramont, 03200 Vichy – tel: 04 70 97 65 06;
email: jacques.decoret@wanadoo.fr

Edgar Dhur and Didier Oudill, page 94
Le Dauphin
167, rue Saint-Honoré, 75001 Paris – tel: 01 42 60 40 11

Éric Frechon, page 76
Le Bristol
112, rue du Faubourg-Saint-Honoré, 75008 Paris –
tel: 01 53 43 43 00; email: resa@hotel-bristol.com;
website: www.hotel-bristol.com

Hervé Galidie, page 180
Le Jardin
37, avenue Hoche, 75008 Paris – tel: 01 42 99 88 00;
email: Hgalidie@aol.com; website: www.royalmonceau.com

Roland et Alexandre Gauthier, page 138
La Grenouillère
La Madeleine-sous-Montreuil, BP 2,
62170 Montreuil-sur-Mer – tel: 03 21 06 07 22;
email: auberge.de.la.grenouillere@wanadoo.fr;
website: www.lagrenouillere.fr

Benoît Guichard, pages 102 and 132
Jamin
32, rue de Longchamps, 75016 Paris –
tel: 01 45 53 00 07

Hans Haas, page 114
Tantris
7 Johann-Fichte Strasse, 80805 Schwabing (Germany) –
tel: (49) 089 361 95 90; email: tantris@t-online.de

Fatema Hal, page 124
Mansouria
11, rue Faidherbe, 75011 Paris – tel: 01 43 71 00 16

Arnold and Alex Hanbuckers, pages 90 and 152
Auberge Herborist
De Watermolen 15, 8200 Bruges (Belgium) –
tel: 50 38 76 00

Patrice Hardy, page 154
email: Patchef.hardy@free.fr

Alberto Herraîz, page 140
Fogon Saint-Julien
10, rue Saint-Julien-le-Pauvre, 75005 Paris –
tel: 01 43 54 31 33; website: www.fogon.fr

Pierre Hermé, page 182
Pierre Hermé
72, rue Bonaparte, 75006 Paris – tel: 01 43 54 47 77
In Japan: *Pierre Hermé Paris*
• The New Otani, 4-1 Kioi-cho, Chiyoda-Ku,
Tokyo 102-8578 – tel: 81 3 3221 2924
• 319, Ikspiari 1-4 Maihama, Urayasu-Shi,
Chiba-Ken 279-8529 – tel: 81 (0)4 7305 5655

Éric Kayser, page 112
Boulangerie Kayser
85, boulevard Malesherbes, 75008 Paris – tel: 01 45 22 70 30

Thomas Keller, page 82
The French Laundry
6640 Washington Street, Yountville, CA 94599
tel: 1 (707) 944 2380

Hirohisa Koyama, page 156
Cooking Stages Haru (bureau central)
Harumi Triton 2F, 1-8-2 Harumi Chuo-ku, Tokyo 104-0053
(Japan) – tel: 81 3 5547 0239

Taïra Kurihara, page 162
Taïra
10, rue des Acacias, 75017 Paris – tel: 01 47 66 74 14;
email: tairacuisinedelamer@hotemail.com

Ursula Makhlouf-Galidie, page 116
email: Umakhlouf@aol.com

Valentino Marcattillii, page 126
Ristorante San-Domenico
Via Gaspare-Sacchi 1, 40026 Imola (Italy) –
tel: (39) 0542 29 000; website: www.sandomenico.it

Régis Marcon, page 92
Auberge Clos-des-Cimes
43290 Saint-Bonnet-le-Froid –
tel: 04 71 59 93 72; email: contact@regismarcon.fr;
website: www.regismarcon.fr

Kiyomi Mikuni, page 128
Hotel Mikuni
1-18 Wakaba, Shinjuku-ku, Tokyo 160-0011 (Japan) –
tel: 81 3 335 138 10

Alain Passard, page 104
L'Arpège
84, rue de Varenne, 75007 Paris –
tel: 01 45 51 47 33; email: arpege.passard@wanadoo.fr;
website: www.alain-passard.com

Paul Pairet, page 184
email: paulpairet@hotemail.com

Brigitte Rakoczy, page 96
La Marée normande
16 *bis*, rue Saint-Denis, 92700 Colombes –
tel: 01 47 82 78 18

Joan Roca, page 164
El Celler de Can Roca
Carretera Tállala 40, 17007 Gijón (Spain) –
tel: (34) 972 22 21 57

Santi Santamaría, page 98
Raco de Can Fabes
Sant-Joan 6, 08470 Sant-Celoni (Spain) –
tel: (34) 93 867 28 51; email: racocanfabes@troc.es;
website: www.racocanfabes.com

Jeffrey Steingarten, page 106
email: jeffrey@vog.com

Michel Troisgros, pages 134 and 142
Troisgros
Place de la Gare, 42300 Roanne – tel: 04 77 71 66 97;
email: troisgros@avo.fr; website: www.troisgros.fr

Charlie Trotter, page 166
Charlie Trotter
816 West Armitage Avenue, Chicago, IL 60614
tel: 773 248 6228; website: www.charlietrotters.com

Luisa Valazza, page 118
Al Sorriso
Via Roma 18, 28018 Soriso (Italy) –
tel: (39) 0322 98 32 28; email: sorriso@alsorriso.com

Jean-Georges Vongerichten, page 168
Jean-Georges
One Central Park West, New York, NY 10023
tel: (212) 299 39 01; website: www.jean-georges.com

Nach Waxman, page 78
Kitchen Arts & Letters
1435 Lexington Avenue, New York, NY 10128
tel: (212) 876 5550

Seak Chan Wong, page 130
La Mer de Chine
159, rue Château-des-Rentiers, 75013 Paris –
tel: 01 45 84 22 49

Bibliography

Splendour and Misery

Balzac H – le Médecin de campagne, in *la Comédie humaine*, Omnibus, Paris, 1999.

Baqué JF – *la Conquête des Amériques* XVe-XVIe *siècle*, Perrin, Paris, 1991.

Bennassar B – *Histoire des Espagnols* VIe-XXe *siècle*, Bouquins, Robert Laffont, Paris, 1992.

Braudel F – *Civilisations matérielles, économie et capitalisme* XVe-XVIIIe *siècle*, Armand Colin, Paris, 1979 ; 3 vol.

– *l'Identité de la France*, Arthaud-Flammarion, Paris, 1986.

Chaunu P et Escamilla M – *Charles Quint*, Arthème Fayard, Paris, 2000.

Graves Ch (editor) – *The Potato Treasure of the Andes*, CIP, Lima, 2001.

Hawkes JG et Fransico-Ortega J – The Potato in Spain during the late 16th Century, *Economic Botany* 1992 ; 46 : 86-97.

Lang J – *Notes of a Potato Watcher*, Texas A & M University Agriculture Series, 2001.

Martinez Shaw C (editor) – *Séville* XVIe *siècle*, Autrement, Série Mémoires, Paris,1992 ; 15.

Métraux A – *les Incas*, Le Seuil, Points-Histoire, Paris, 1983.

Oke OL (editor) – Roots, Tubers, Plantains and Bananas, in *Human Nutrition*, FAO, Rome, 1990.

Salaman R – *The History and Social Influence of the Potato*, Cambridge University Press, Cambridge, 1989.

Serres (de) O – *le Theatre d'agriculture et mesnage des champs*, Actes Sud, Thesaurus, Arles, 1996.

Watchel N – *la Vision des vaincus*, Gallimard, Folio-Histoire, Paris, 1971.

Potato Garden

Ochoa CM – *las Papas de Sudamerica, Peru*, CIP, Lima, 2001.

Stein S – *My Weeds, A Gardener's Botany*, University Press of Florida, 2000.

Reading List

Auberge Herborist
Arnold Hanbuckers, Lannoo, Terra, Gent, 2002.

Bras Laguiole Aubrac France
Michel and Sébastien Bras, Éditions du Rouergue, Rodez, 2002.

El Bulli, 1998-2002
Ferràn Adrià, El Bulli Books, Roses, 2002.

Charlie Trotter's Vegetables
Charlie Trotter, Ten Speed Press, Berkeley, California, 1996.

Chocolate Desserts by Pierre Hermé
Dorie Greenspan, Little Brown, New York, 2001.

La Cuisine vagabonde
Jean-Philippe Derenne, Fayard-Mazarine, Paris, 1999.

Éloge de la cuisine française
Édouard Nignon, Éditions Fançois Bourin, Paris, 1992.

The French Laundry Cookbook
Thomas Keller, Artisan, New York, 1999.

Fresh from the Garden
Perla Myers, Clarkson Potter Publishers, New York, 1996.

Le Gourmand des quatre saisons
Bénédict Beaugé, Nil Éditions, Paris, 1999.

Le Guide culinaire
Auguste Escoffier, Flammarion, Paris, 1921.

El Gusto de la diversidad, el Mundo cucinario
Santi Santamaria, Everest, León, 2002.

It Must 've been Something I Ate
Jeffrey Steingarten, Knopf, New York, 2002.

Kulinarishe Skizzen
Hans Haas, Fischer-Pipenbrock, Munich, 2002.

Le Livre de cuisine
Jules Gouffé, Parangon, Paris, 2001.

The New Food Lovers Tiptionary
Sharon Tyler Herbst, Morrow, New York, 2002.

Saveurs du Japon
Hirohisa Koyama et Marianne Comolli, Albin Michel, Paris, 1998.

Simple to Spectacular
Jean-Georges Vongerichten & Marc Bittman, Broadway Books, New York, 2000.

Shunju – New Japanese Cuisine
Takashi Sugimoto and Marcia Iwatate, Periplus, Singapore, 2002.

Sushi & Susci
Moreno Cedroni, Bibliotheca Culinaria, Lodi, 2000.

Address Book

Association de la Bleue de Borée
Mairie de Borée, 07310 Borée
Tel/fax: + 33 (0)4 75 29 10 87
Website: www.boree.fr.st
To order Bleue de Borée potatoes (a rare and forgotten variety that needs rediscovering) and to keep the post office going in this little village in the Ardèche (mail orders of 5kg)

Carroll's Heritage Potatoes Limited
Tiptoe Farm
Cornhill-on-Tweed
Northumberland TD12 4XD
Tel/Fax: 01890 883060
Website: www.heritage-potatoes.co.uk
Growers and suppliers of gourmet varieties of heritage potatoes, offering unique cooking qualities, special flavour, interesting colours and shapes, giving the consumer a taste of history.

Charlton Park Garden Centre
Charlton Road
Wantage
Oxfordshire
OX12 8EP
Tel: 01235 772700
Fax: 01235 760414
Website: www.charlton-park.co.uk
Over 120 varieties of seed potatoes including Roseval, Ratte, Franceline, Mona Lisa and Samba, can be purchased direct or on line

CIP (International Potato Centre)
PO Box 1558, Lima 12, Peru
Tel: + (51-4) 349-6017
Email: cip@cgiar.org
Website: www.cipotato.org
For further information about the world of the potato

ISSA (Irish Seed Savers Association)
Capparoe
Scariff
Co Clare
Ireland
Tel: 00353 61 921866
Fax: 00 353 61 921397
Website: www.irishseedsavers.ie
Have around 30 heritage varieties on the seed potato list

Organic Gardening Catalogue
Riverdene Business Park
Molesey Road
Hersham
Surrey KT12 4RG
Tel: 01932 253666
Fax: 01932 252707
Website: www.organiccatalogue.com
Seed potatoes and heritage microplants

Specialist Potatoes Ltd
George M Sinclair
8 Provost Park
Auchtermuchty
Fife KY14 7DT
Tel: 01337 828645
Email: george@specialistpotatoes.co.uk
Website: www.specialistpotatoes.co.uk
Specialists in sourcing and producing unusual (especially red and blue fleshed) and conservation potatoes including organic Charlotte

SEED SWAPS
Every variety of seed sold in the UK these days needs an official EU licence, which can cost several thousand pounds. So many varieties, which do not have universal commercial appeal get neglected and become in fact illegal. Anyone can help to keep these valuable old and local varieties going by joining the increasing network of seed swappers, which aims to grow these varieties and keep our genetic seed heritage as rich as possible.

North Devon Seed Swap
http://seedswap.mysite.wanadoo-members.co.uk

Brighton Seed Swap
www.seedysunday.org

International Network
www.primalseeds.org

Tamar Organics
Tavistock Woodlands Estate
Gulworthy
Tavistock
Devon PL19 8DE
Tel: 01822 834887
Fax: 01822 834284
Website: www.tamarorganics.co.uk
All organic varieties of seed potatoes including Bintje and Belle de Fontenay

Tuckers Seeds
Brewery Meadow
Stonepark
Ashburton
Newton Abbot
Devon TQ13 7DG
Tel: 01364 652233
Fax: 01364 654211
email: seeds@edwintucker.com
Website: http://www.edwintucker.com
Over 80 varieties of seed potatoes including Ratte and 11 heritage microplants

Acknowledgements

Grant Symon, for bringing *Potato* up front.
Ursula Makhlouf-Galidie, for accompanying us on the potato trail from Paris to Lima.
Béatrice Weité, our literary coach and editor who lives in Avenue Parmentier in Paris -, for her sleepless nights and infallible eye.
Alan Romans 'Mister Potato', the Scottish keeper of the potato in Europe.
Nach Waxman, who never forgot to share his latest discoveries with us every time we visited his bookshop.
Hervé Galidie, for making the recipes more palatable reading.
Pierre Hermé and his insatiable serenity.
Charles Znaty and the Socrepa House for their invaluable advice.
Annick and Dominique Hisbergue, for going part way with us.
Ginette and Michel Bras, for their photos of studious holidays.
Baptiste Kieken, our trusty photographic assistant, for his vigilance.
Christophe Auger, aka 'speedy type', and Artyg, for their commitment.
The Anselm family, from Colombes and Colombia, for the Colombian potato.
M. and Mme Michel Renard: go and see them on Wednesday and Saturday in the Maisons-Laffitte market and try their organic vegetables and armfuls of seasonal produce.
Joël Thiébault, a big-hearted market gardener and foodie, into everything and a fan of potatoes, tomatoes, beetroots, radishes, cucumbers, roots and herbs. You can find him at the Marché de l'Alma market on Wednesday and Saturday.
Richard Ledu, for his Japonaiseries and insatiable curiosity.
Christine Graves of the CIP in Lima, Peru, for her help with the artwork.
Alain Flammarion, Ghislaine Bavoillot, Nathalie Démoulin and Sylvie Ramaut.
Sylvie Amar and Marie-Gabrièle Verdoni for their 'Nuancier Patates'.
Apple France for the computer support they gave *Patate*.
Alexandra Mallet, for his loyalty.
Brodie and Sarah, for their angelic patience.
Arabella and Marguerite, for their patience and hearty appetites.

Air France for its high-flying partnership.

PICTURE CREDITS
Pages 8-9: CIP; p.10: Javier Silva/CIP; p.11: Candelaria Atalaya/CIP; p.12; Franz Frey/CIP; p.13: Michel Bras; p.14: Candelaria Atalaya/CIP; pp.15-16: Michel Bras; p.17: Alejandro Balaguer/CIP; p.18: Bridgeman/Giraudon; p.19 (top): Hispanic Society of America, New York; p.19: (bottom)-p.20 (bottom): Candelaria Atalaya/CIP, Rafael Larco Herrera Archaeological Museum (Lima, Peru), National Museum of Archaeology, Anthropology and History of Peru; p.20 (top): private collection; p.21: Michel Bras; p.22: Bridgeman/Giraudon; p.24: Bridgeman/Giraudon; p.26: Musée Plantin, Antwerp; p.27: Bridgeman/Giraudon; p.28: Grant Symon; p.30: Alejandro Balaguer/CIP; p.33: Bridgeman/Giraudon; pp.34-37: Alejandro Balaguer/CIP; p.45 and flyleaf: Patrick Mikanowski. All other photos in the book and pp.24, 35, 38-44: Grant Symon.

If you loved this book or had an instant reaction, let us know at **www.patate-lelivre.com**

To find out all about Grant Symon: **www.GrantSymon.com**

Published in 2005 by
Grub Street
4 Rainham Close
London
SW11 6SS
Email: food@grubstreet.co.uk
Web: www.grubstreet.co.uk

Translated from the French by Tamsin Black
Edited by Anne Dolamore
First published in French as *Patate* by Flammarion

A catalogue record for this book is available from the British Library

ISBN 1 904943 35 7

SENIOR EDITOR
Ghislaine Bavoillot

ARTISTIC DIRECTOR
Patrick Mikanowski

GRAPHIC DESIGN
Dominique Hisbergue

ARTWORK AND PRODUCTION MANAGER
Ursula Maklhouf-Galidie

EDITOR
Nathalie Démoulin

EDITORIAL COORDINATION
Béatrice Weité